THE OFFICAL

LIFE IS STRANGE

COLORING BOOK

SQUARE ENIX.

TITAN COMICS

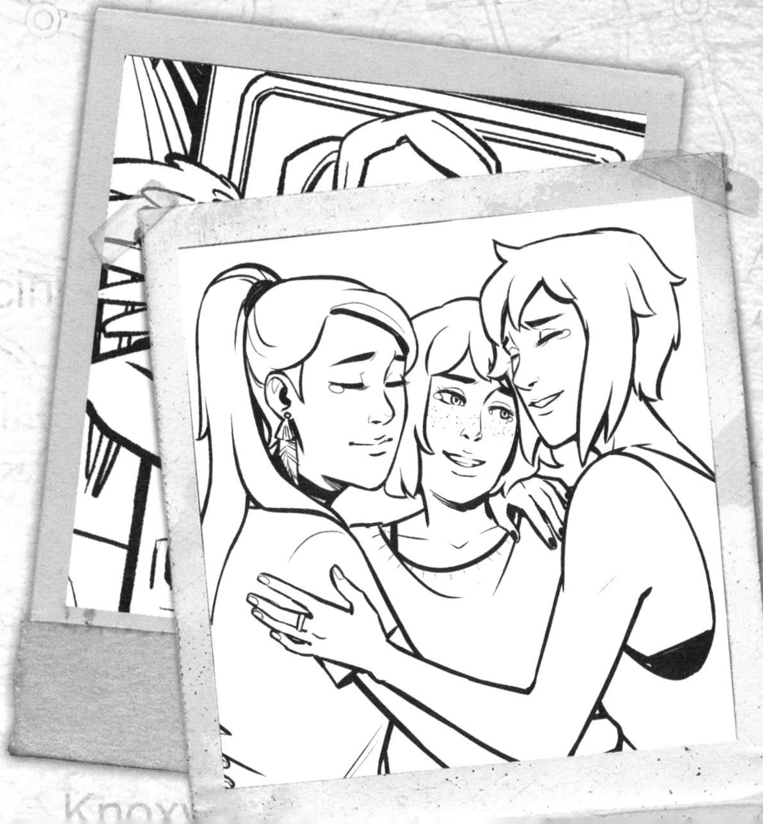

LIFE IS STRANGE

EDITOR
PHOEBE HEDGES

DESIGNER
DONNA ASKEM

TITAN COMICS

GROUP EDITOR
JAKE DEVINE

PRODUCTION MANAGER
JACKIE FLOOK

PUBLICIST
WILL O'MULLANE

PUBLISHING DIRECTOR
JOHN DZIEWIATKOWSKI

EDITORIAL ASSISTANT
CALUM COLLINS

ART DIRECTOR
OZ BROWNE

DIGTIAL & MARKETING MANAGER
JO TEATHER

PUBLISHING DIRECTOR
RICKY CLAYDON

SENIOR CREATIVE EDITOR
DAVID LEACH

SALES & CIRCULATION MANAGER
STEVE TOTHILL

HEAD OF RIGHTS
JENNY BOYCE

OPERATIONS DIRECTOR
LEIGH BAULCH

PRODUCTION CONTROLLERS
CATERINA FALQUI & KELLY FENLON

MARKETING COORDINATOR
LAUREN NODING

ACQUISITIONS EDITOR
DUNCAN BAIZLEY

PUBLISHERS
VIVIAN CHEUNG & NICK LANDAU

SPECIAL THANKS
TO JON M BROOKE, SCOTT BLOWS, ANDREW JAMES, ERIN BOWER, AND TO ALL AT SQUARE ENIX.
AND TO JONATHAN ZIMMERMAN AND FELICE KUAN AT DECK NINE GAMES.
SPECIAL THANKS TO THE TEAMS AT DONTNOD AND DECK NINE GAMES.

PUBLISHED BY TITAN COMICS, A DIVISION OF TITAN PUBLISHING GROUP, LTD., 144 SOUTHWARK STREET, LONDON SE1 OUP.
TITAN COMICS IS A REGISTERED TRADEMARK OF TITAN PUBLISHING GROUP, LTD. ALL RIGHTS RESERVED.

A CIP CATALOGUE RECORD FOR THIS TITLE IS AVAILABLE FROM THE BRITISH LIBRARY.

ISBN: 9781787739598
FIRST EDITION: SEPTEMBER 2022
10 9 8 7 6 5 4 3 2 1

PRINTED IN THE UK.

FOR RIGHTS INFORMATION CONTACT JENNY.BOYCE@TITANEMAIL.COM

WWW.TITAN-COMICS.COM
BECOME A FAN ON FACEBOOK.COM/COMICSTITAN
FOLLOW US ON TWITTER @COMICSTITAN

THE OFFICAL

LIFE IS STRANGE
COLORING BOOK

ART BY
CLAUDIA LEONARDI AND IOLANDA ZANFARDINO

ORIGINAL STORY AND CHARACTERS BY
RAOUL BARBET, JEAN-LUC CANO AND MICHEL KOCH.

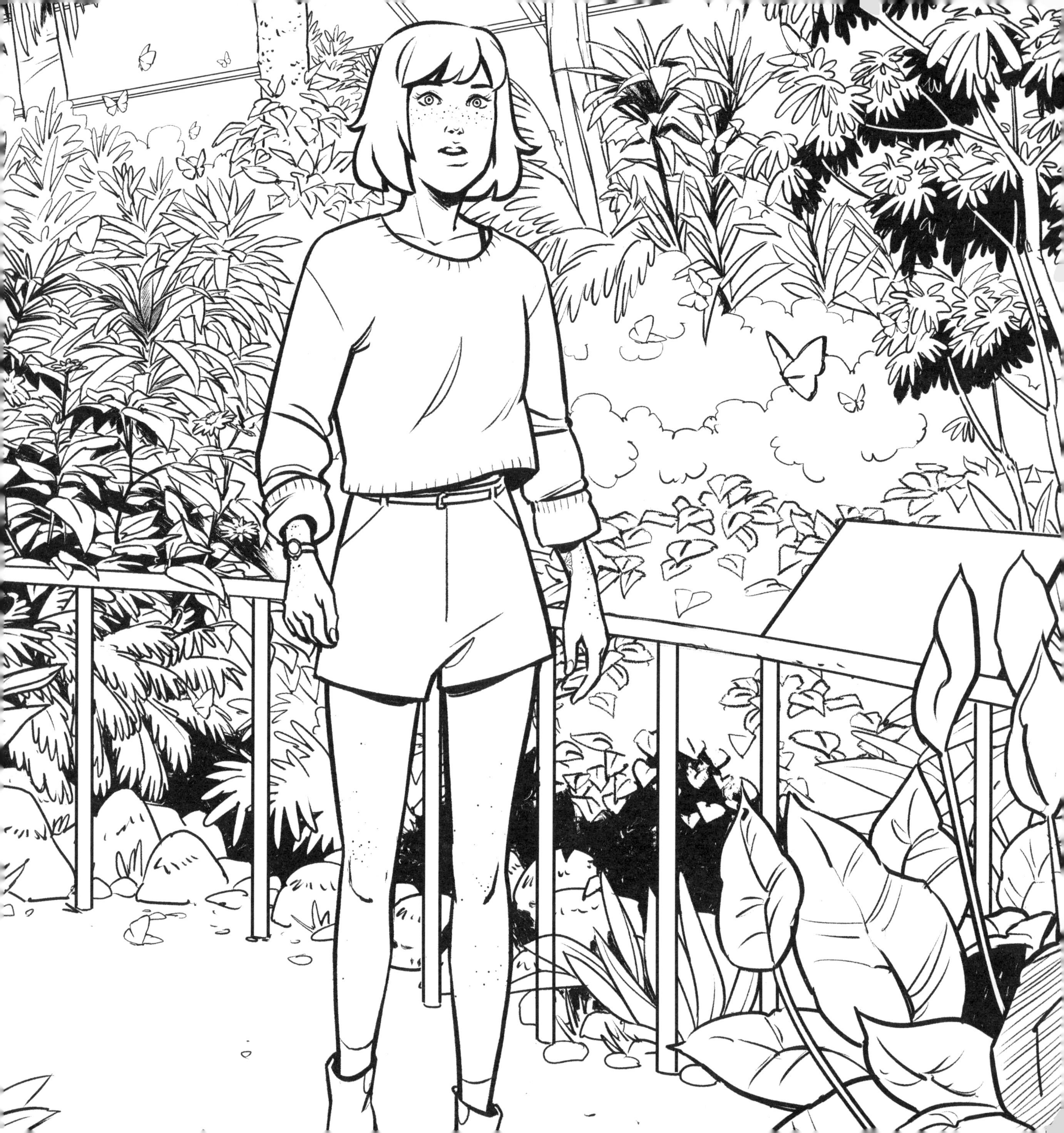

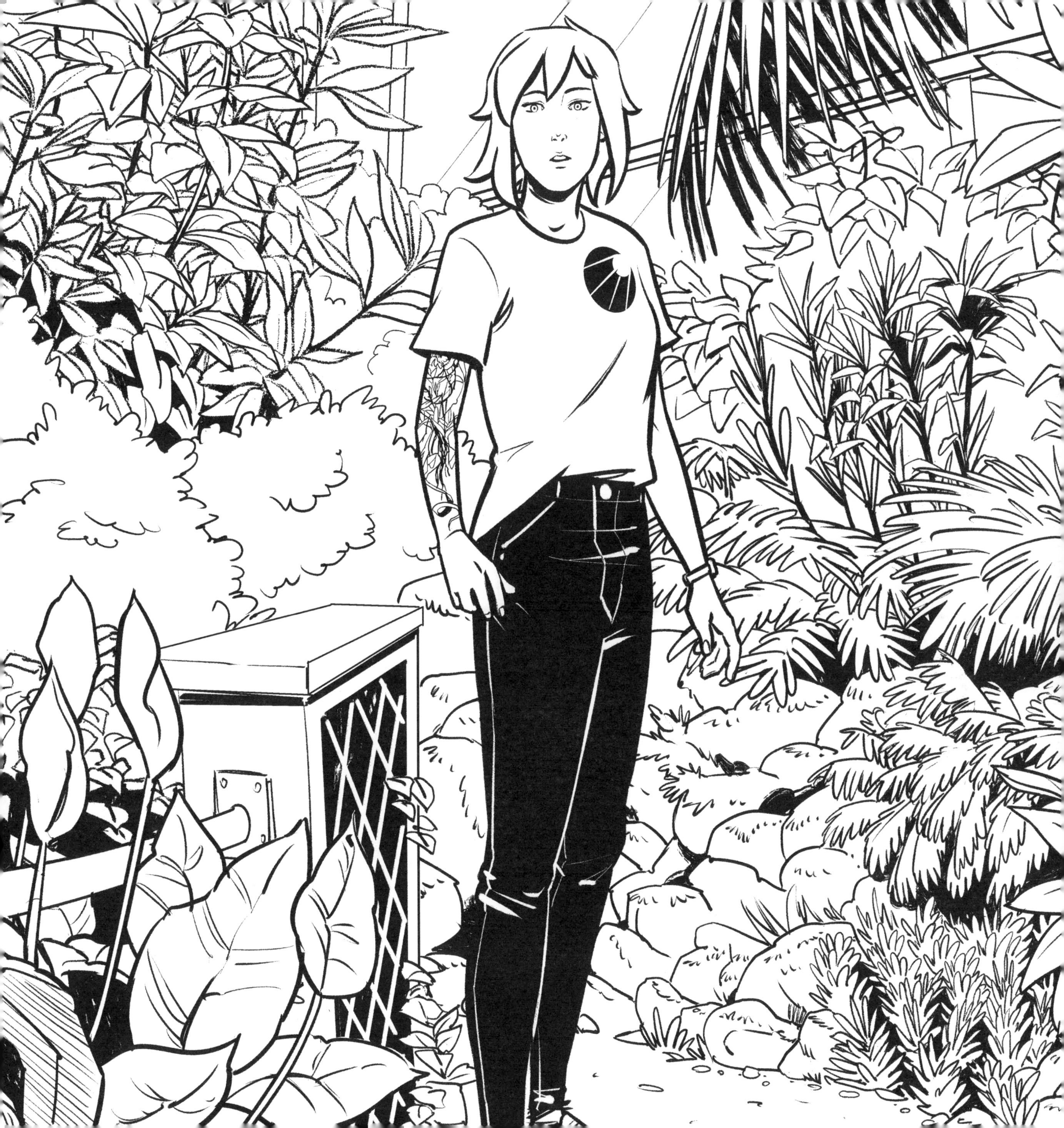

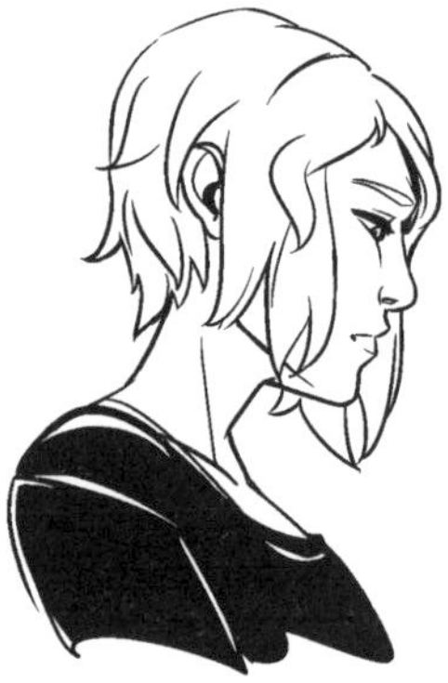

DESIGN CHLOE'S T-SHIRT

Chloe's style made her stand out in the town of Arcadia Bay. From band merch to tour tees, what other t-shirts do you think Chloe keeps in her wardrobe?

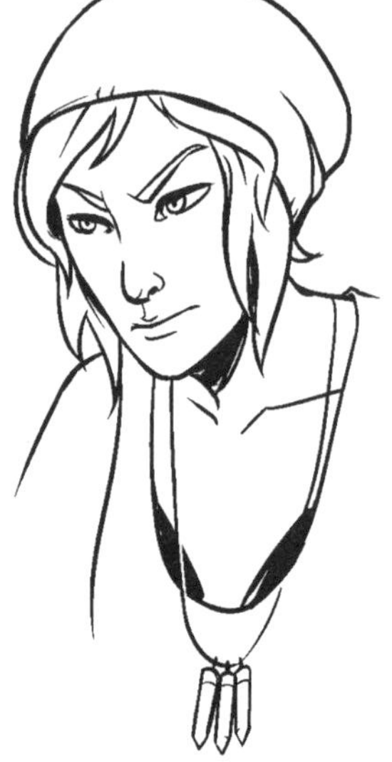

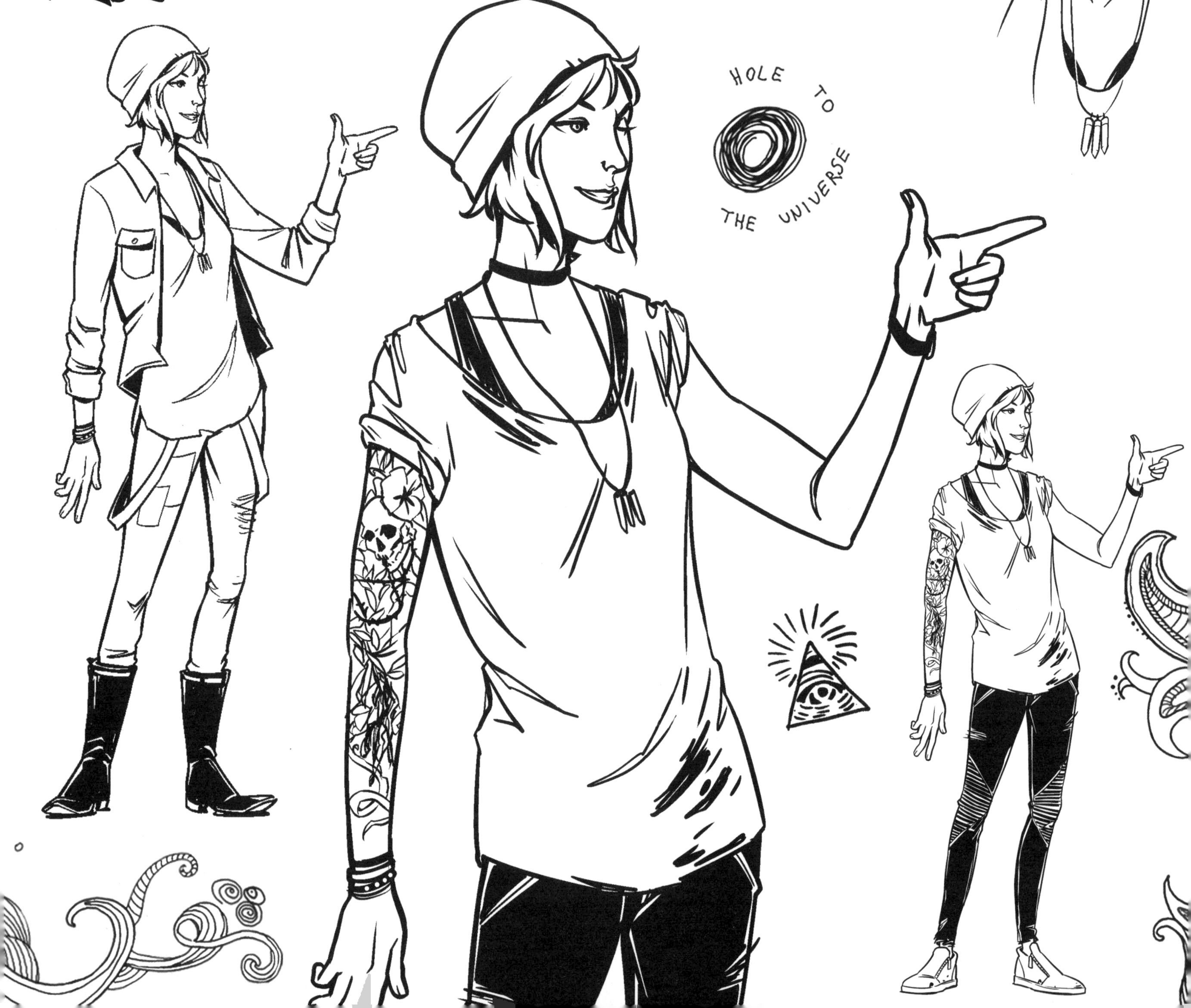
HOLE TO THE UNIVERSE

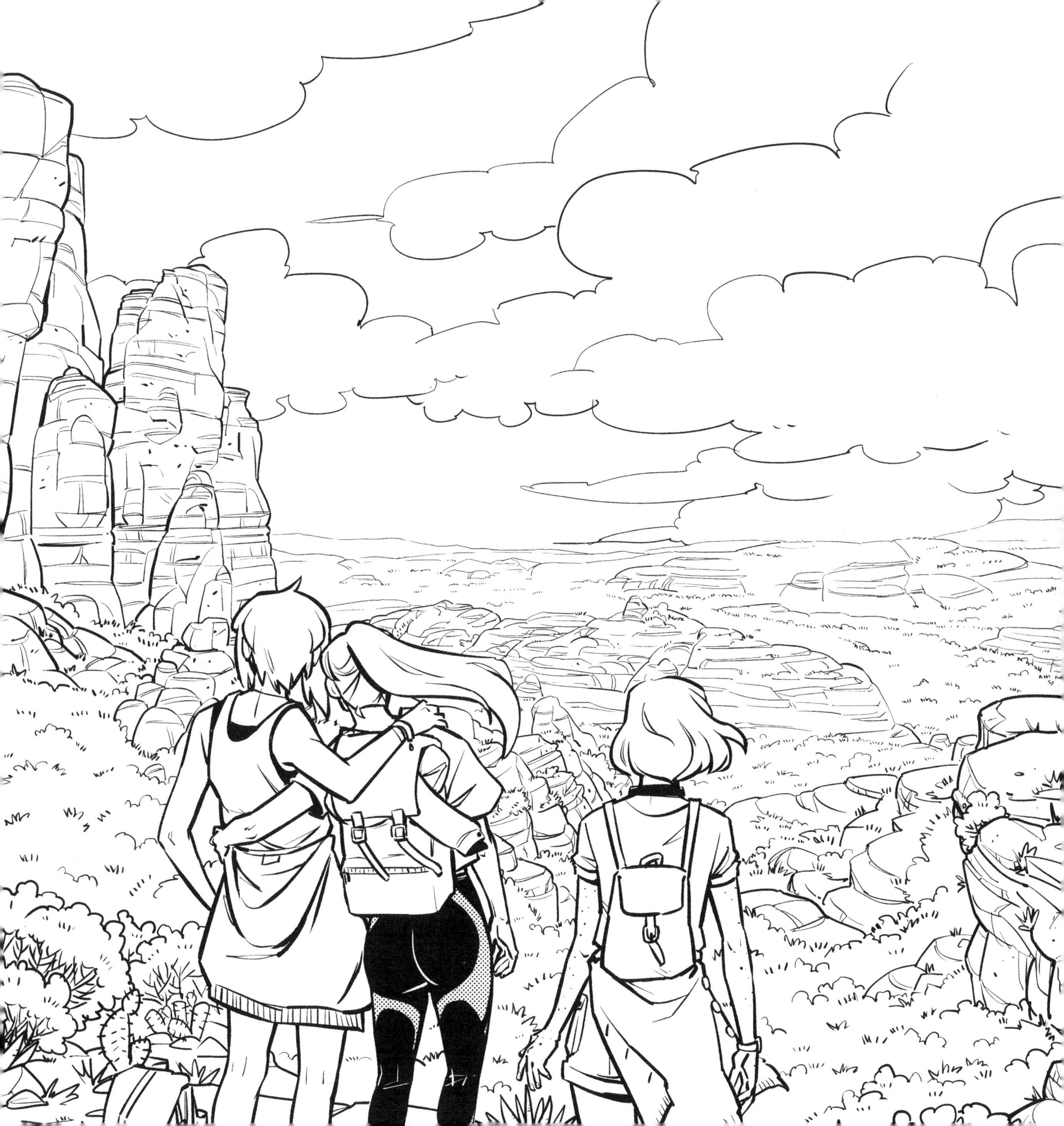

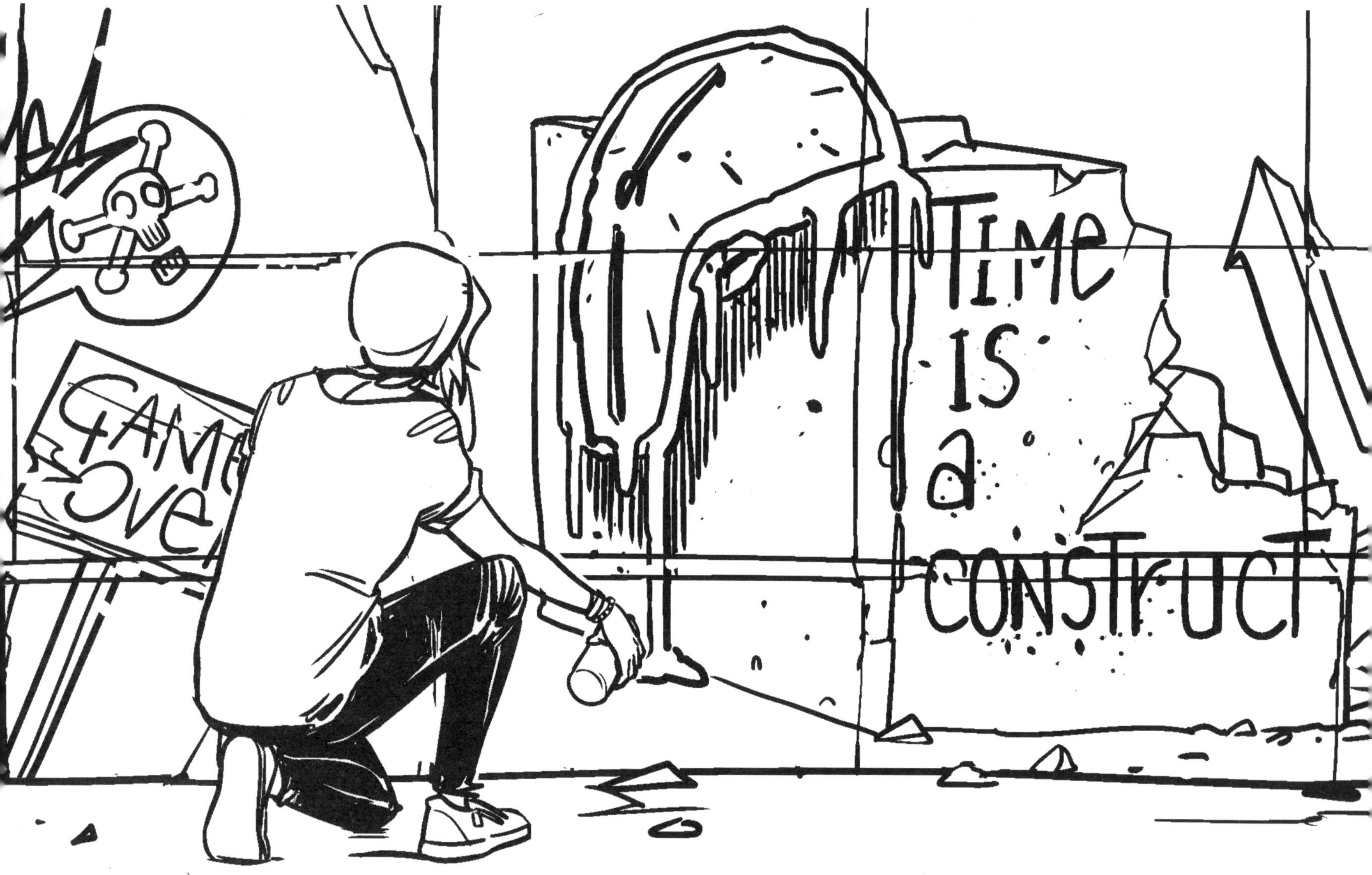
GAME OVE
TIME IS a CONSTRUCT

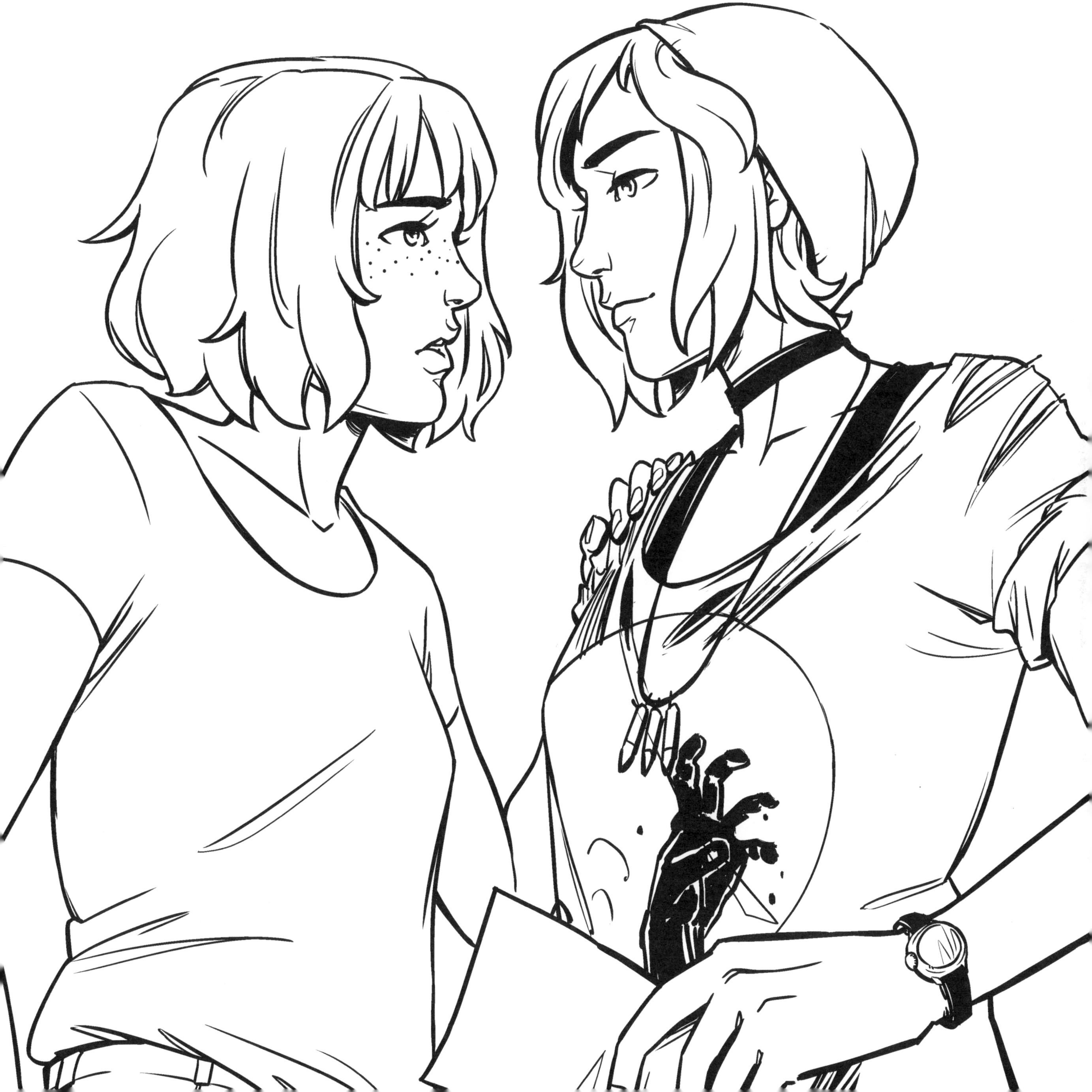

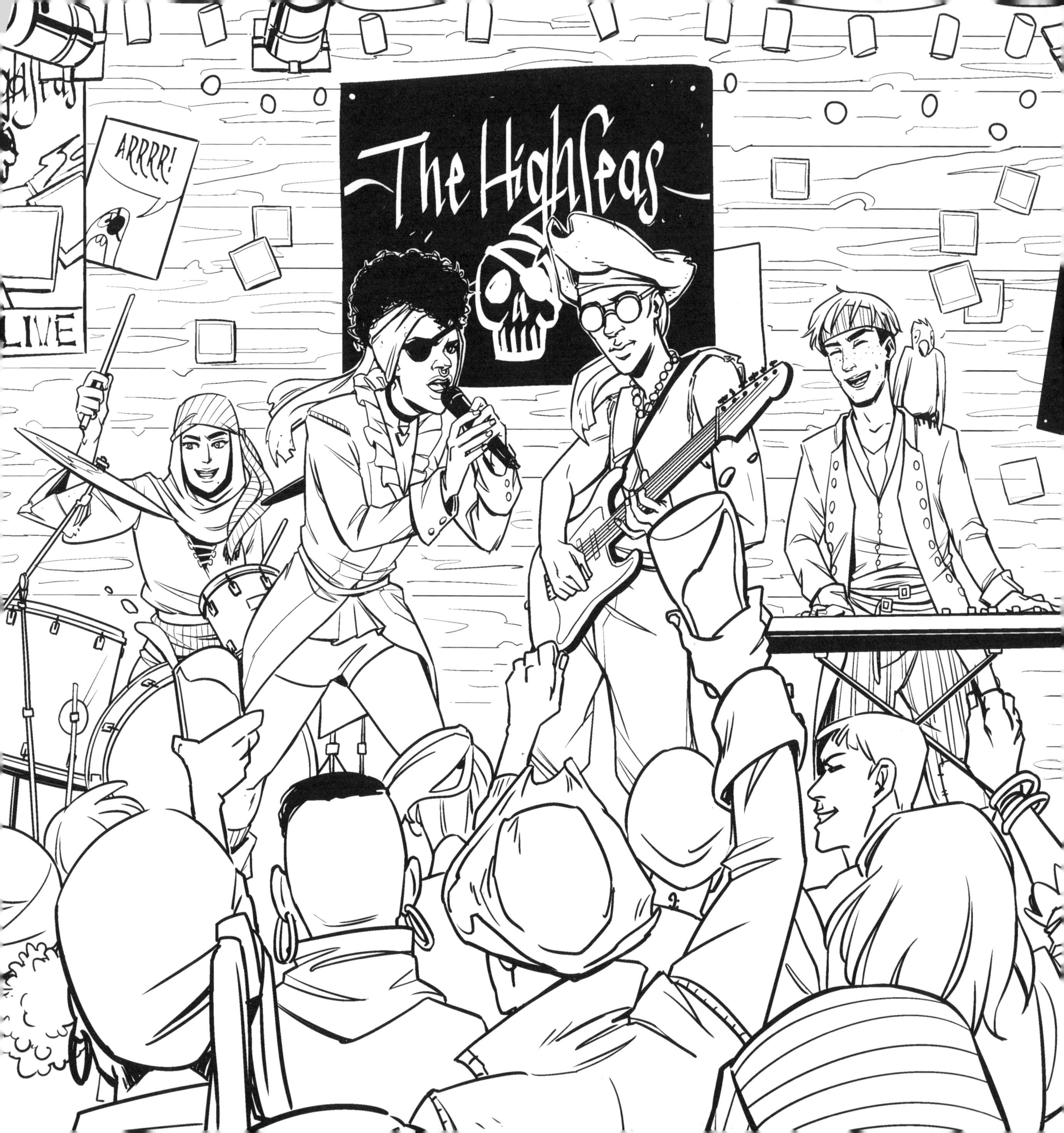
The High Seas
ARRRR!
LIVE

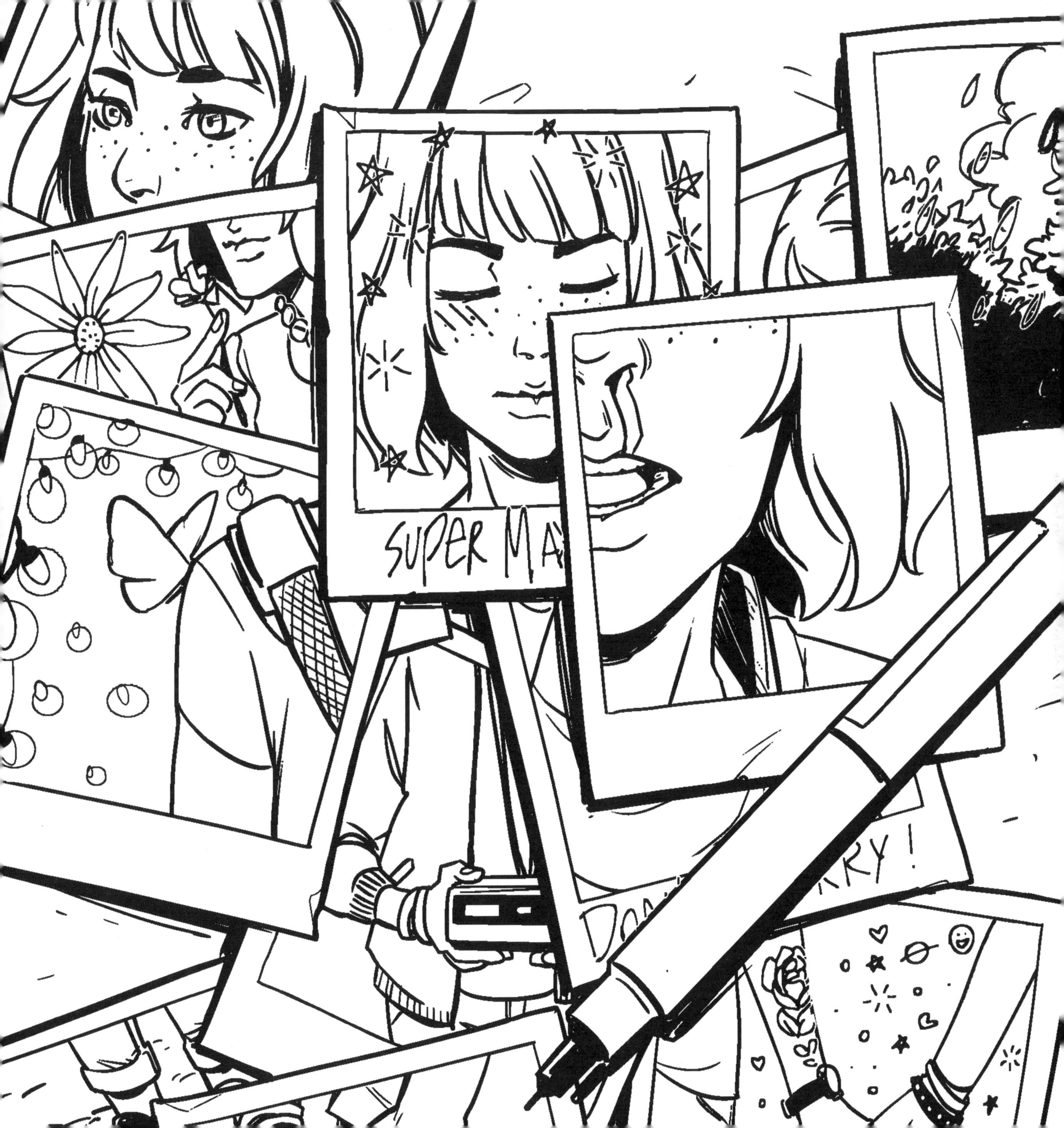
SUPER MA

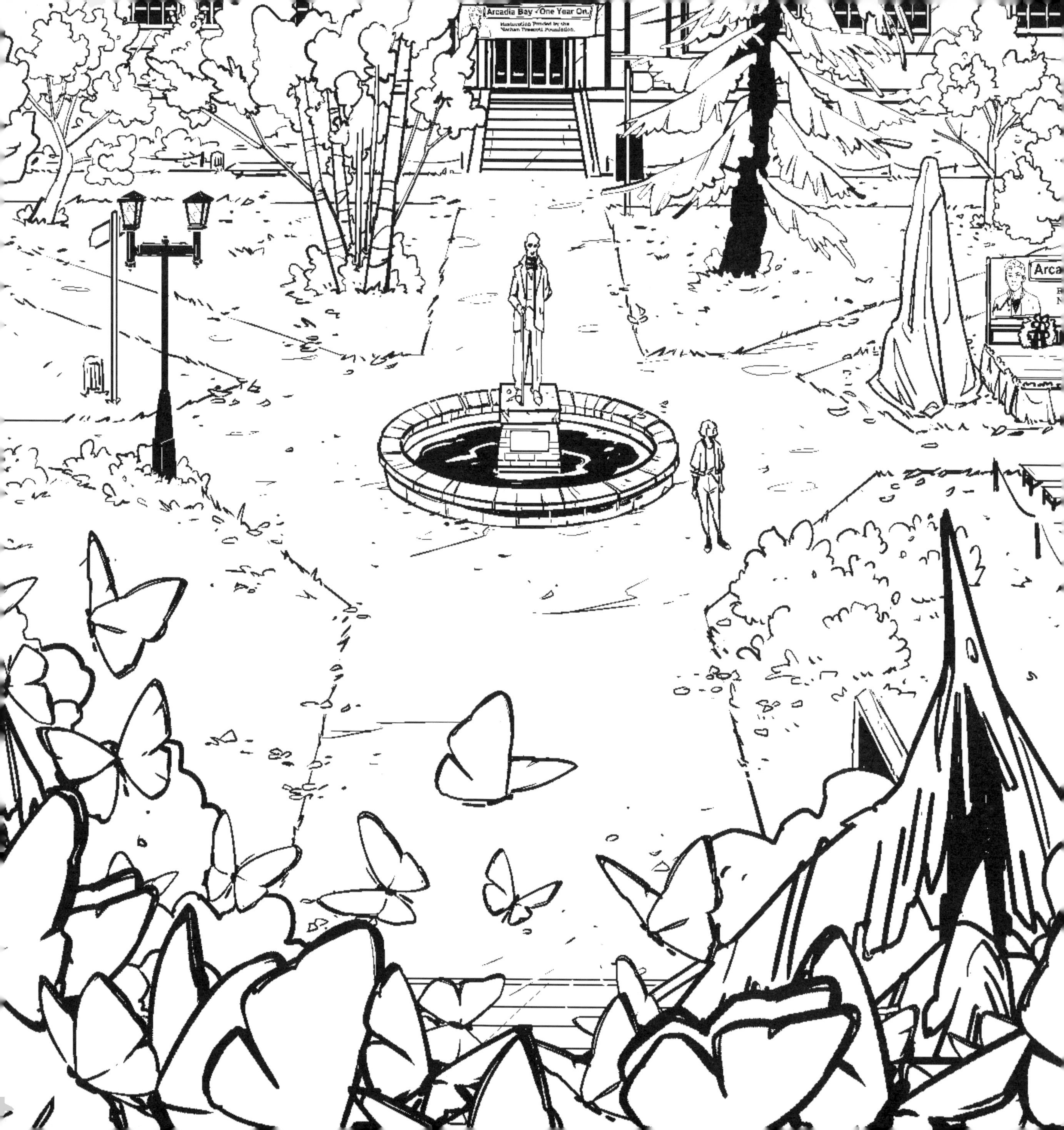
Arcadia Bay - One Year On.

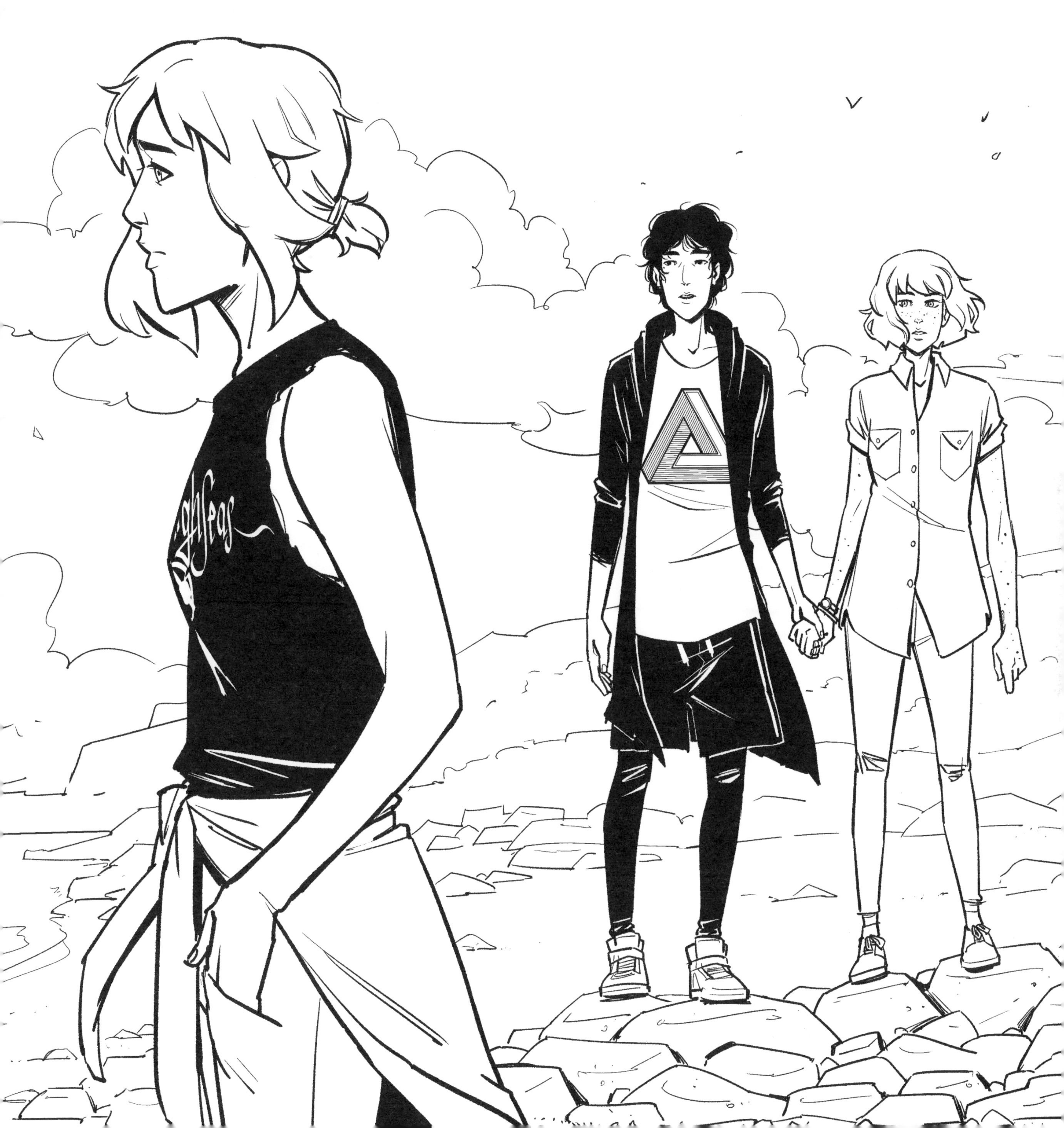

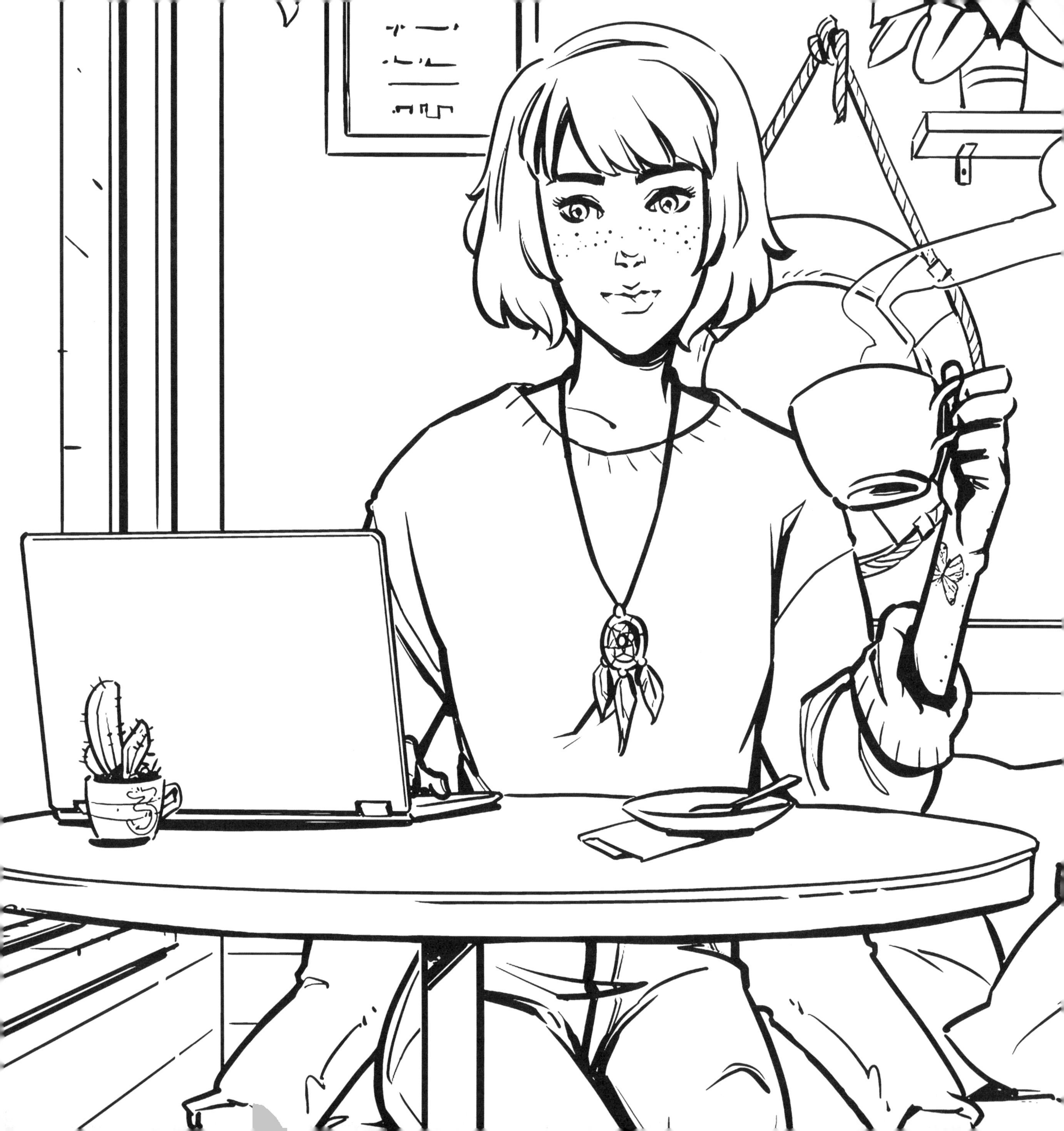

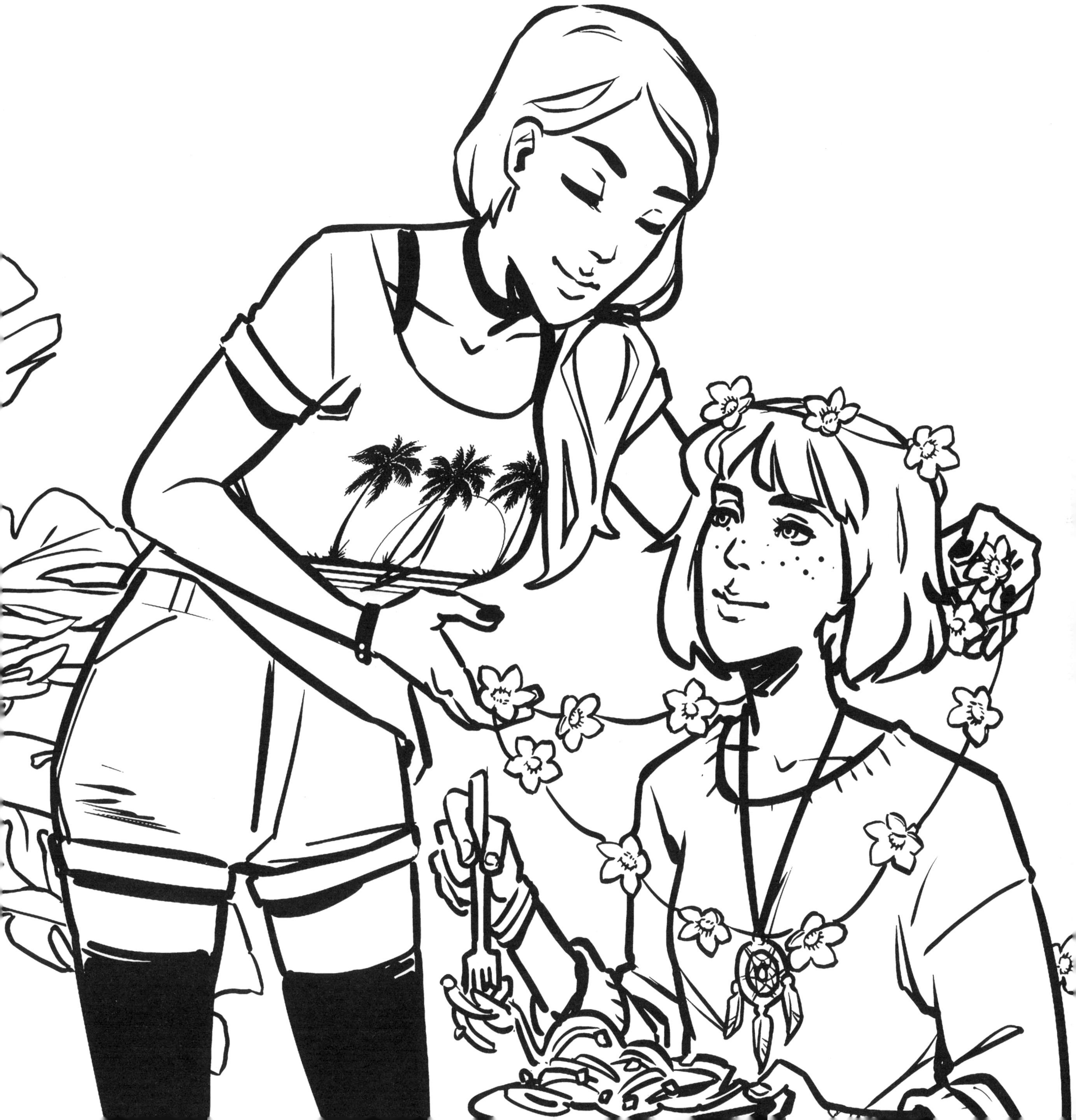

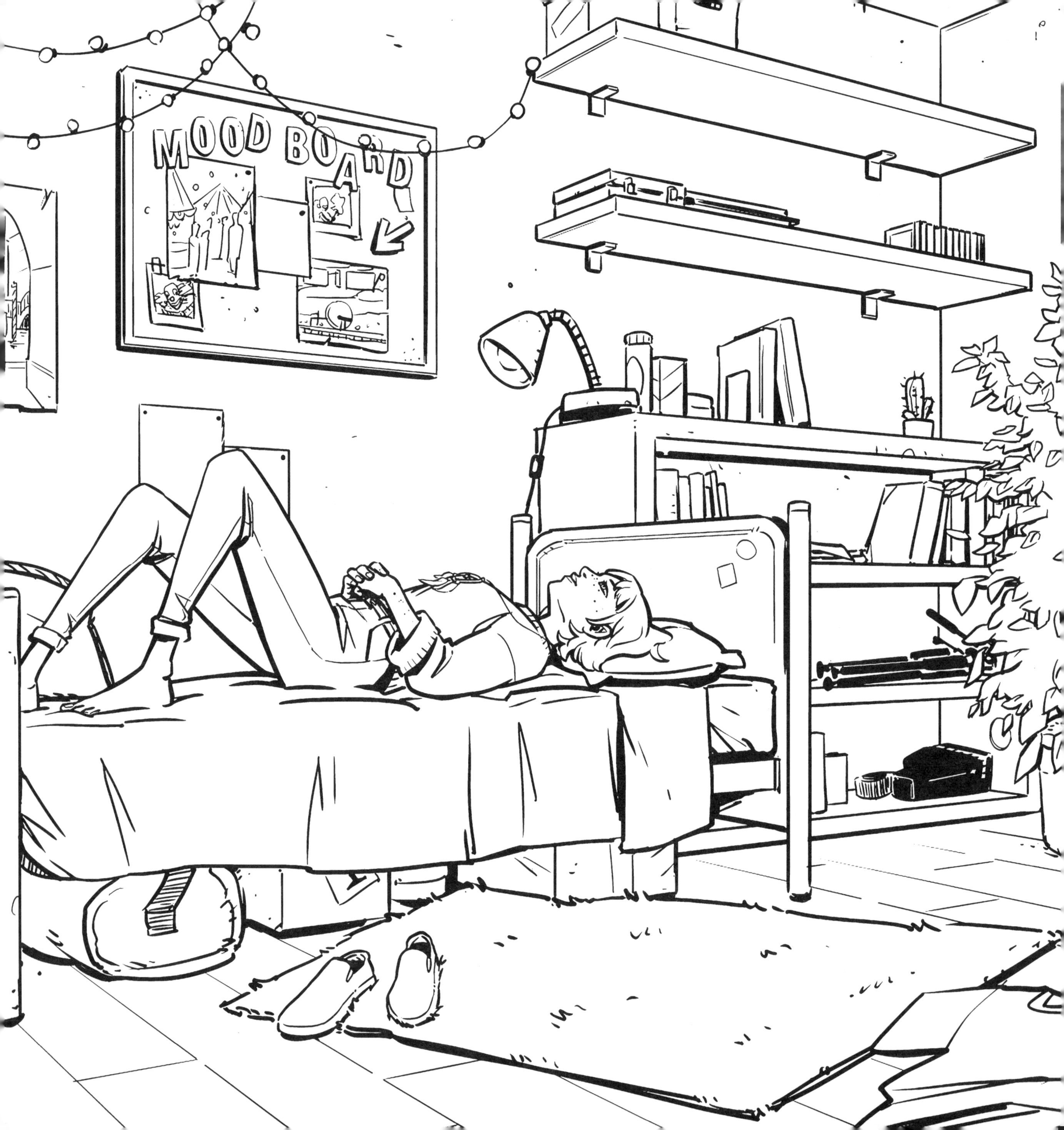
MOOD BOARD

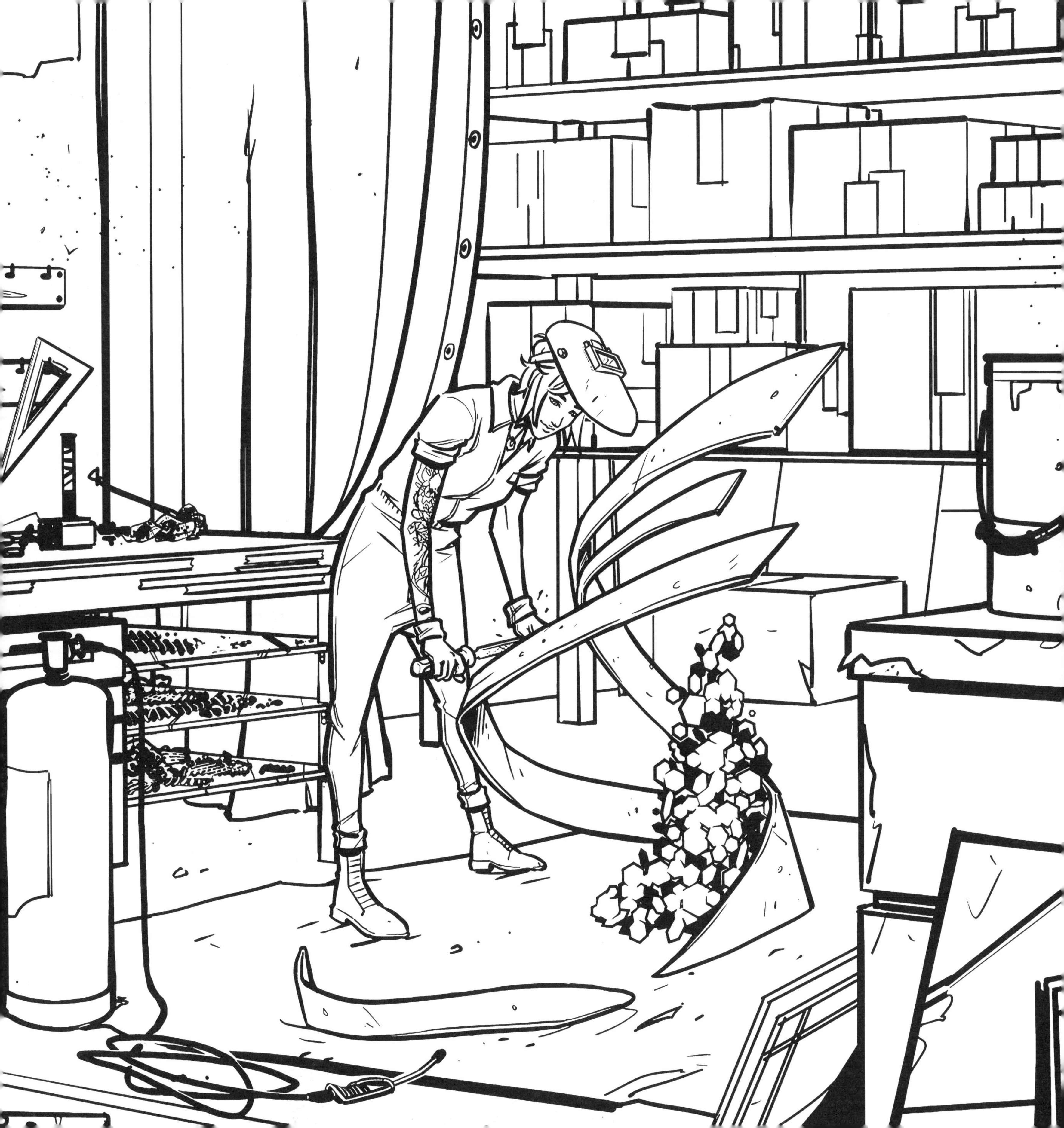

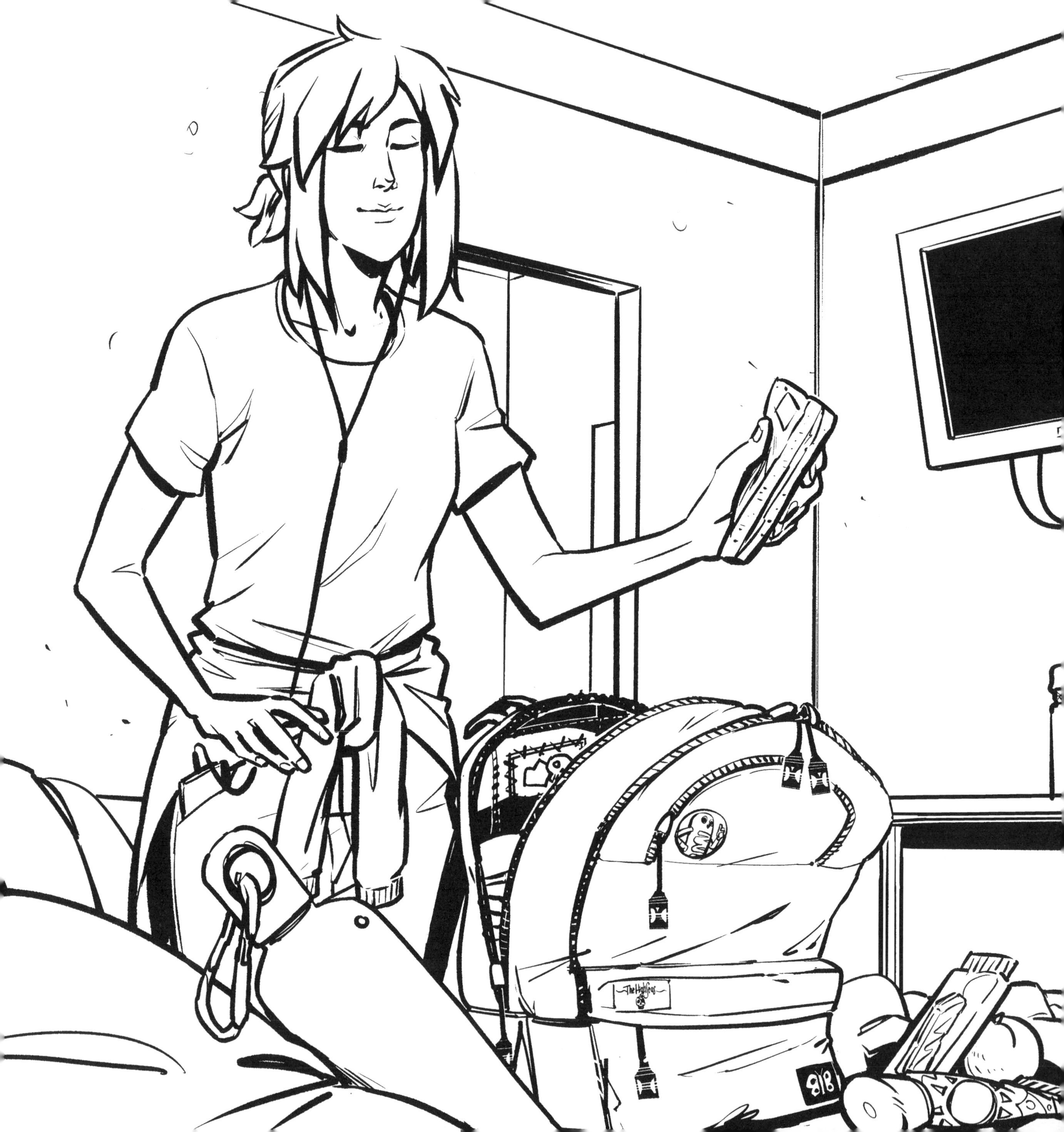
The High Seas

DRAW GLIMPSES OF OTHER TIMELINES

With near-infinite timelines for Max to jump into, no wonder a familiar face might pop up from time to time. Add in your own possibilities for the choices Max could make!

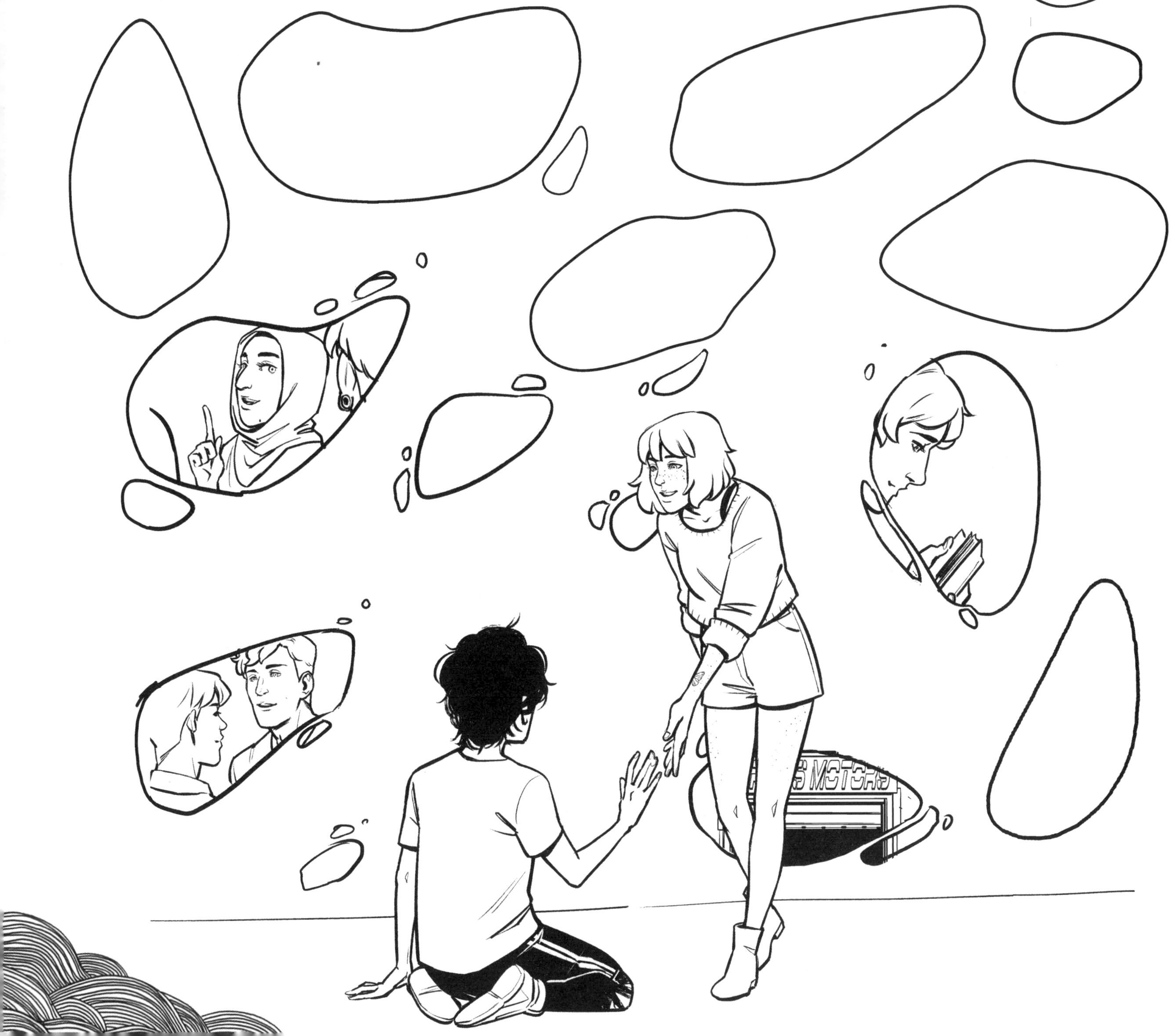

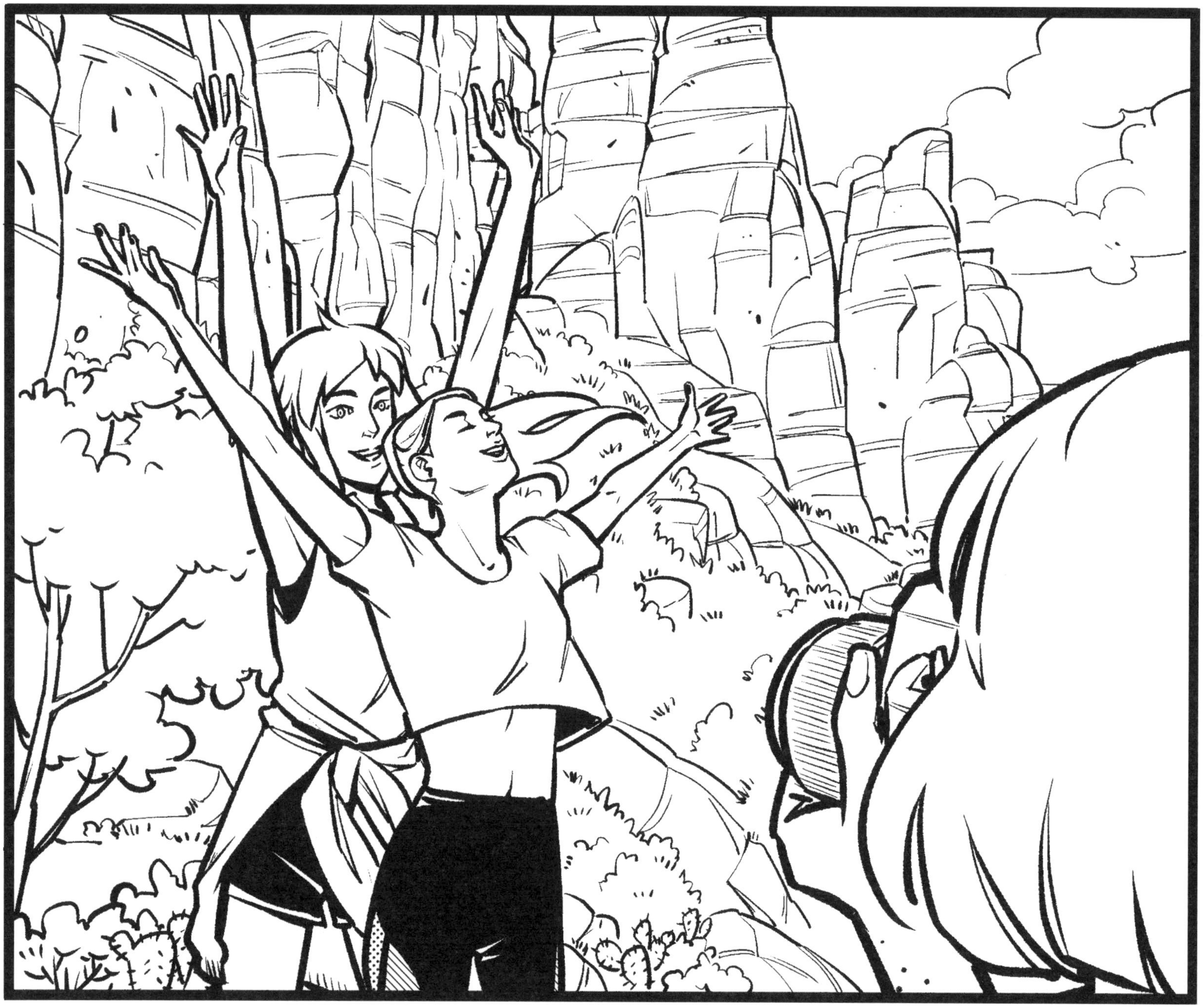

SAY FROMAGE!

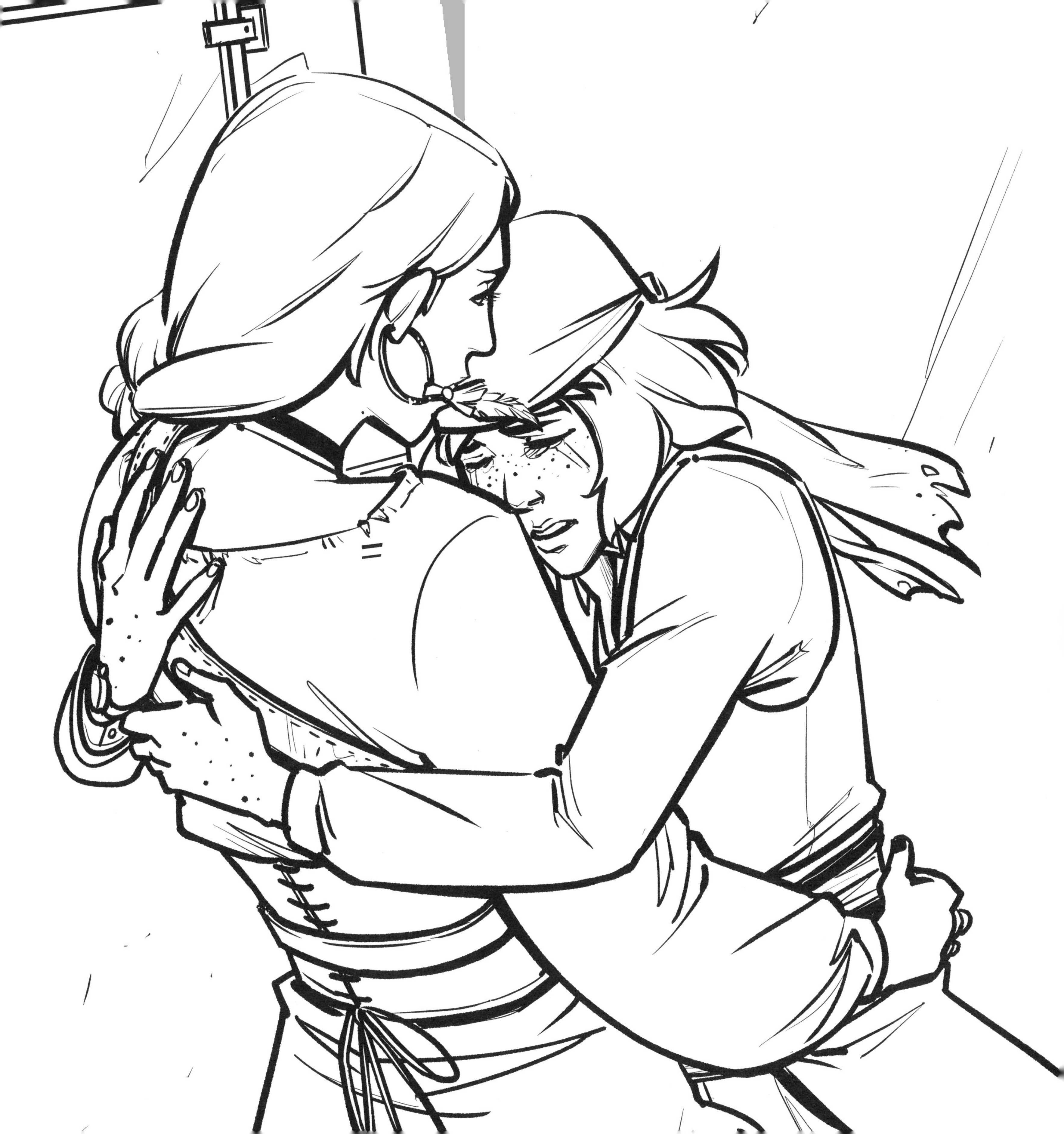

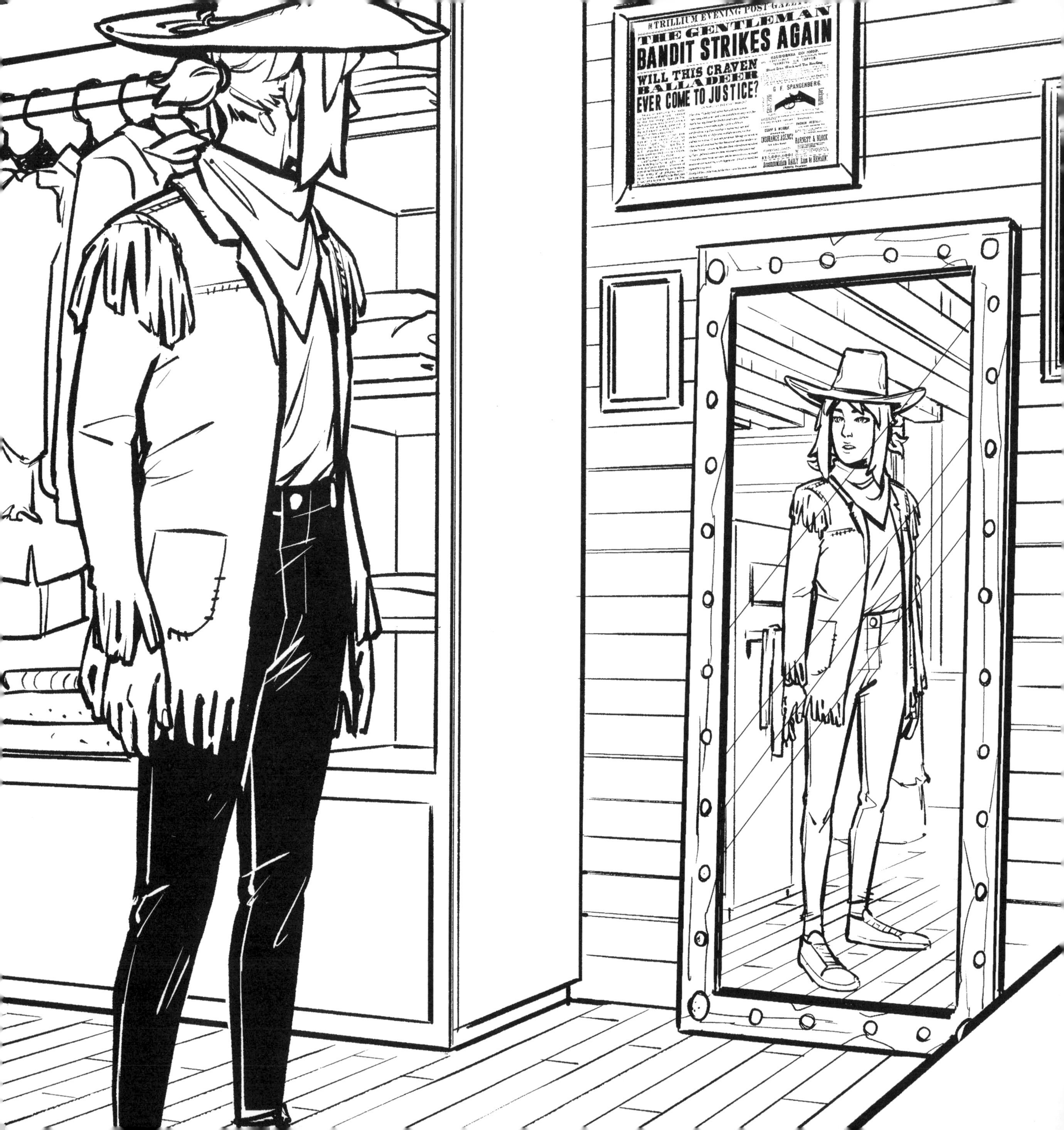
TRILLIUM EVENING POST
THE GENTLEMAN BANDIT STRIKES AGAIN
WILL THIS CRAVEN BALLADEER EVER COME TO JUSTICE?
G. F. SPANGENBERG
INSURANCE AGENCY
BARNETT & BLOCK

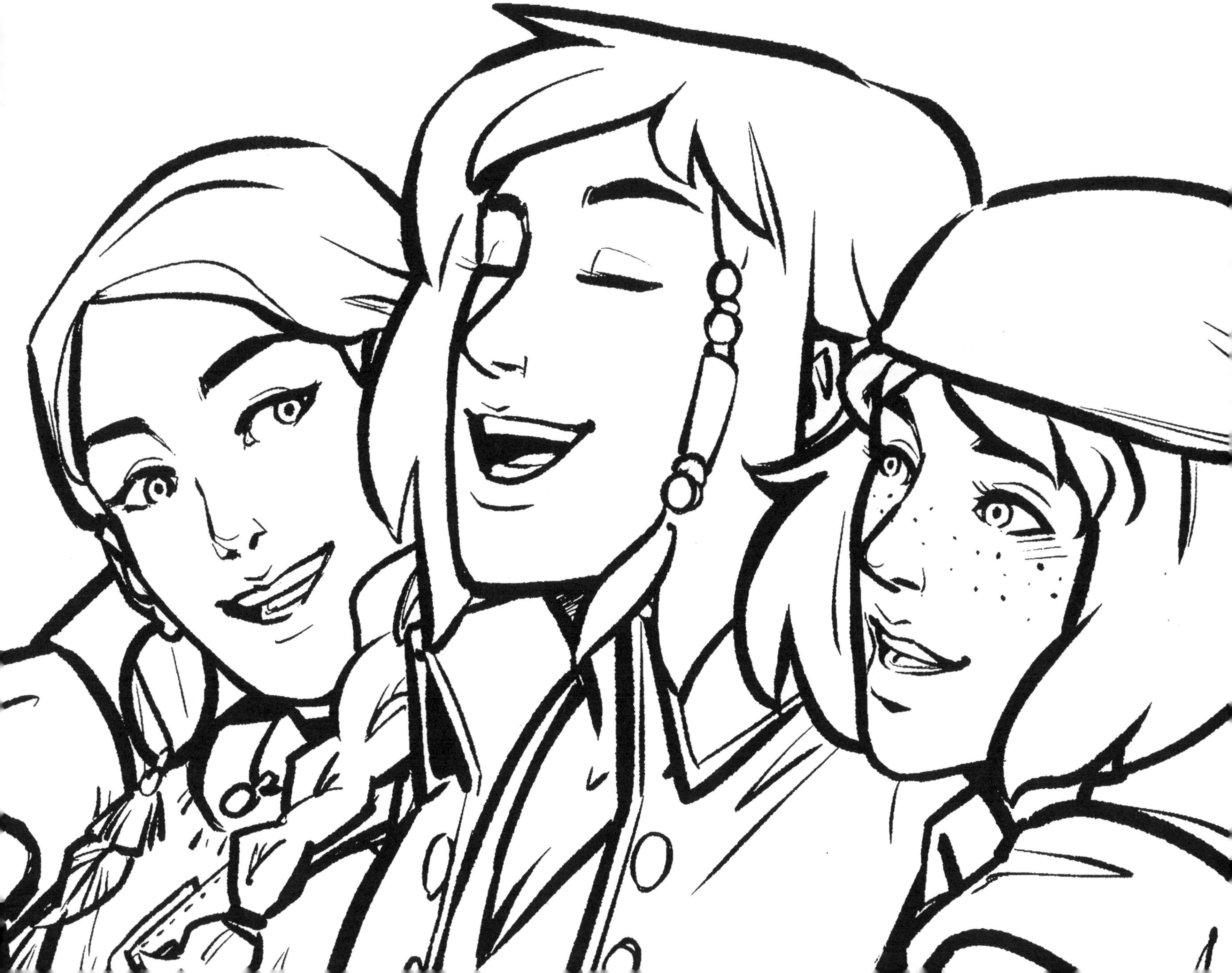

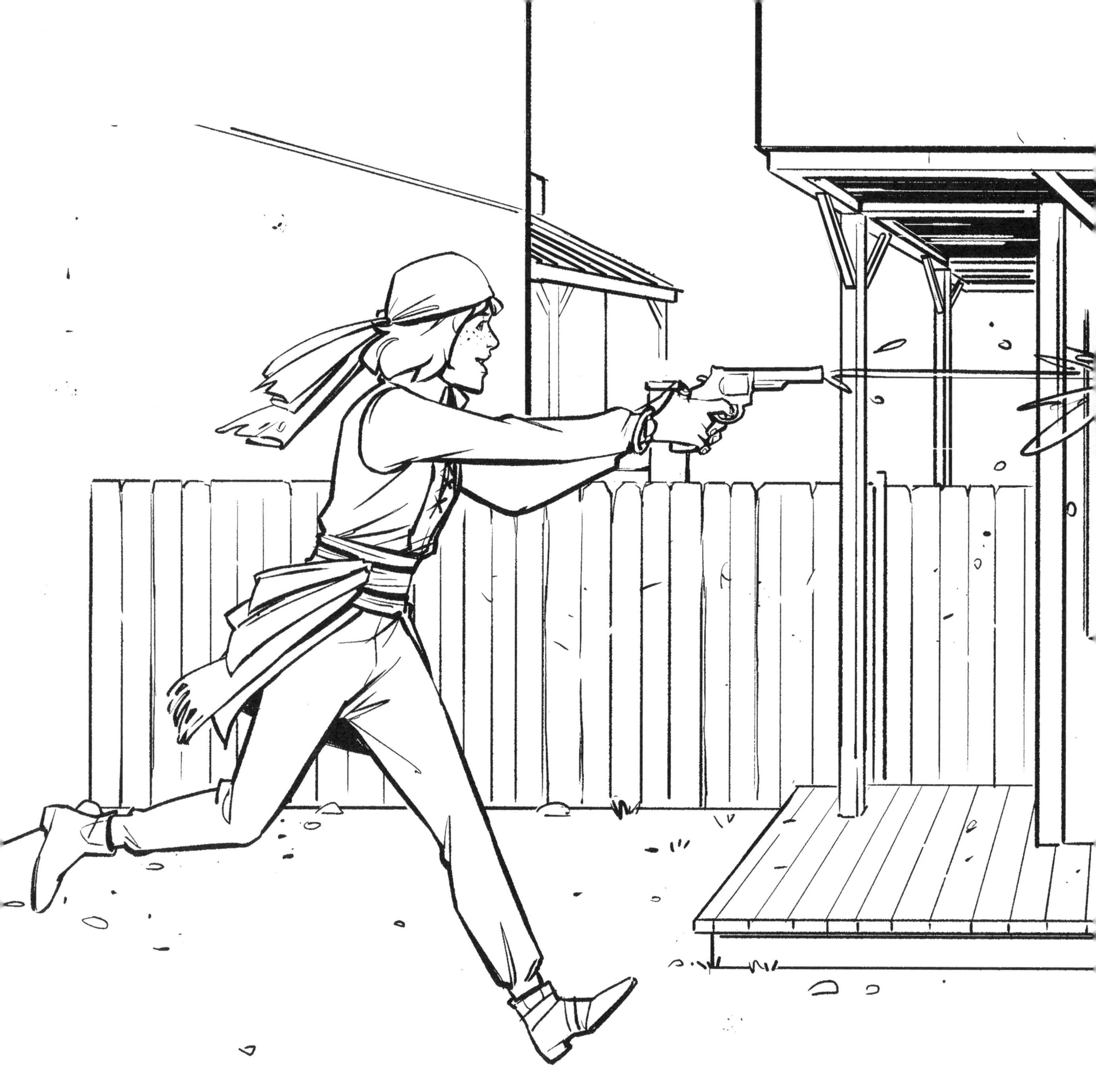

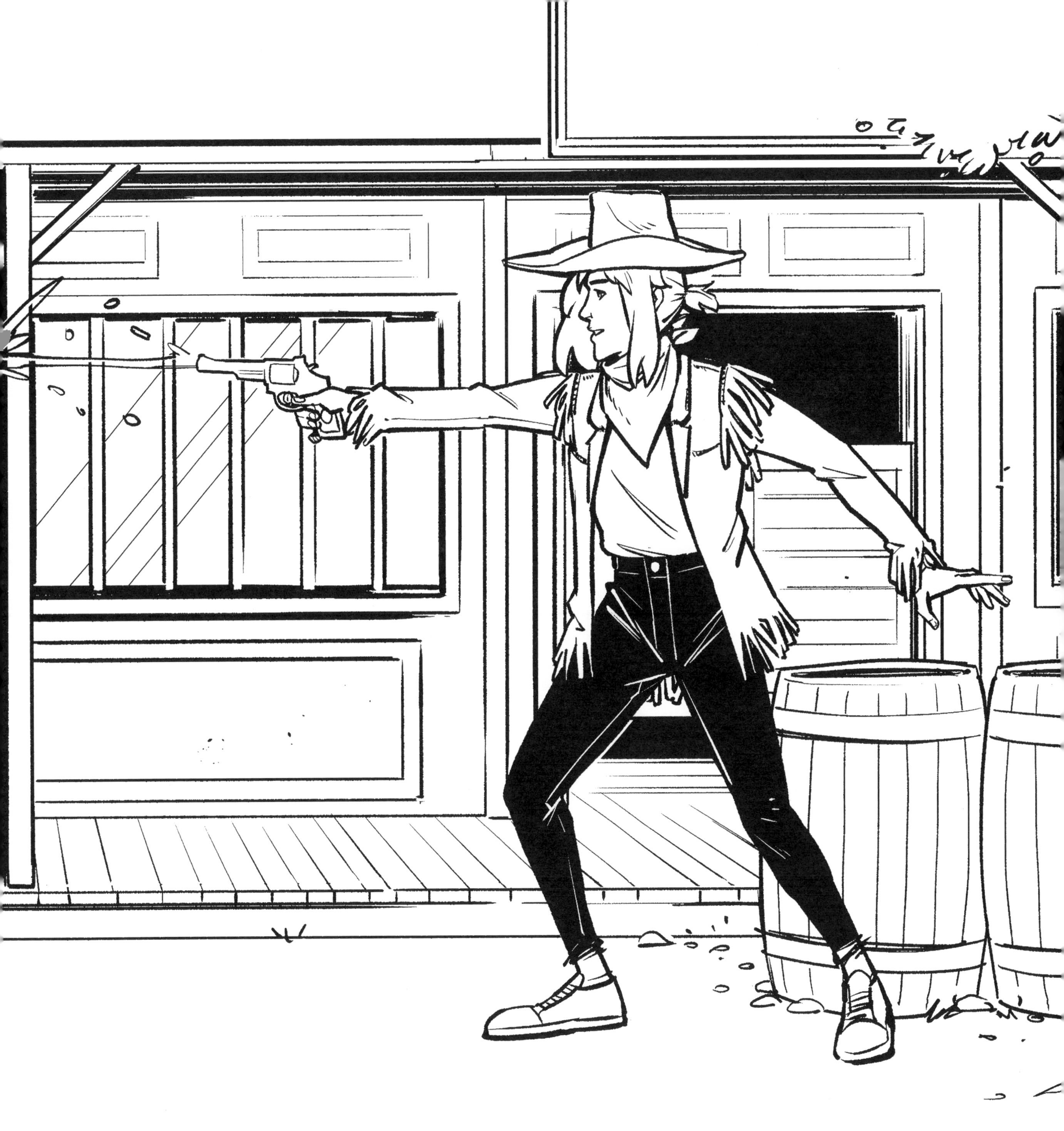

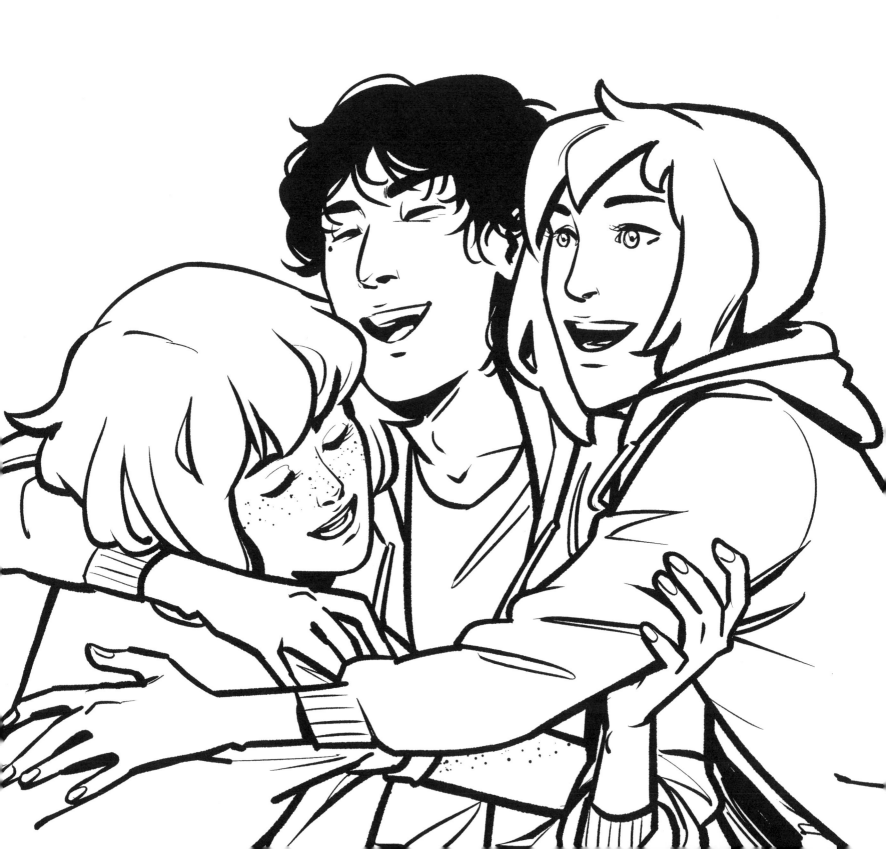

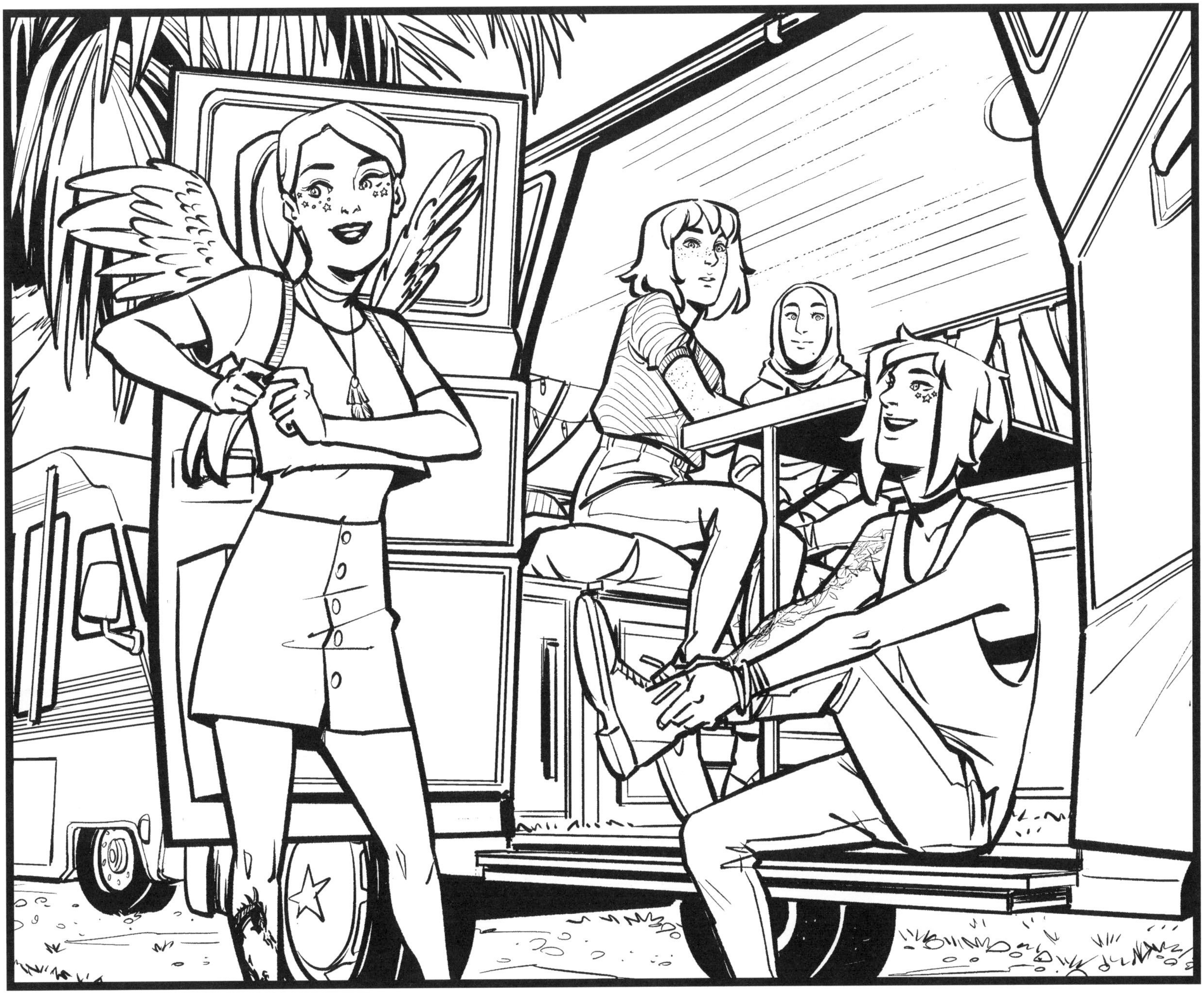

NEW ORLEANS, 2016

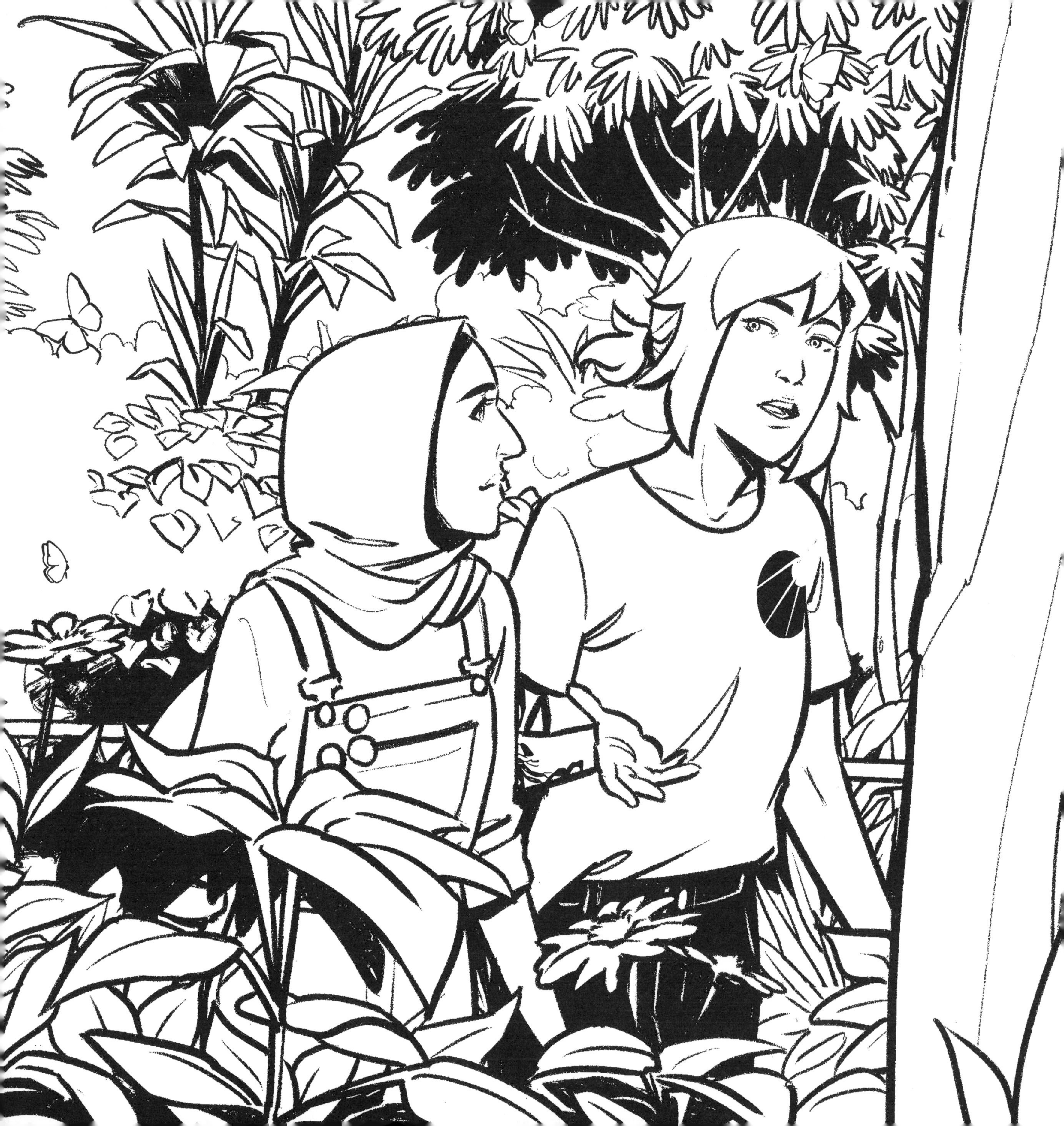

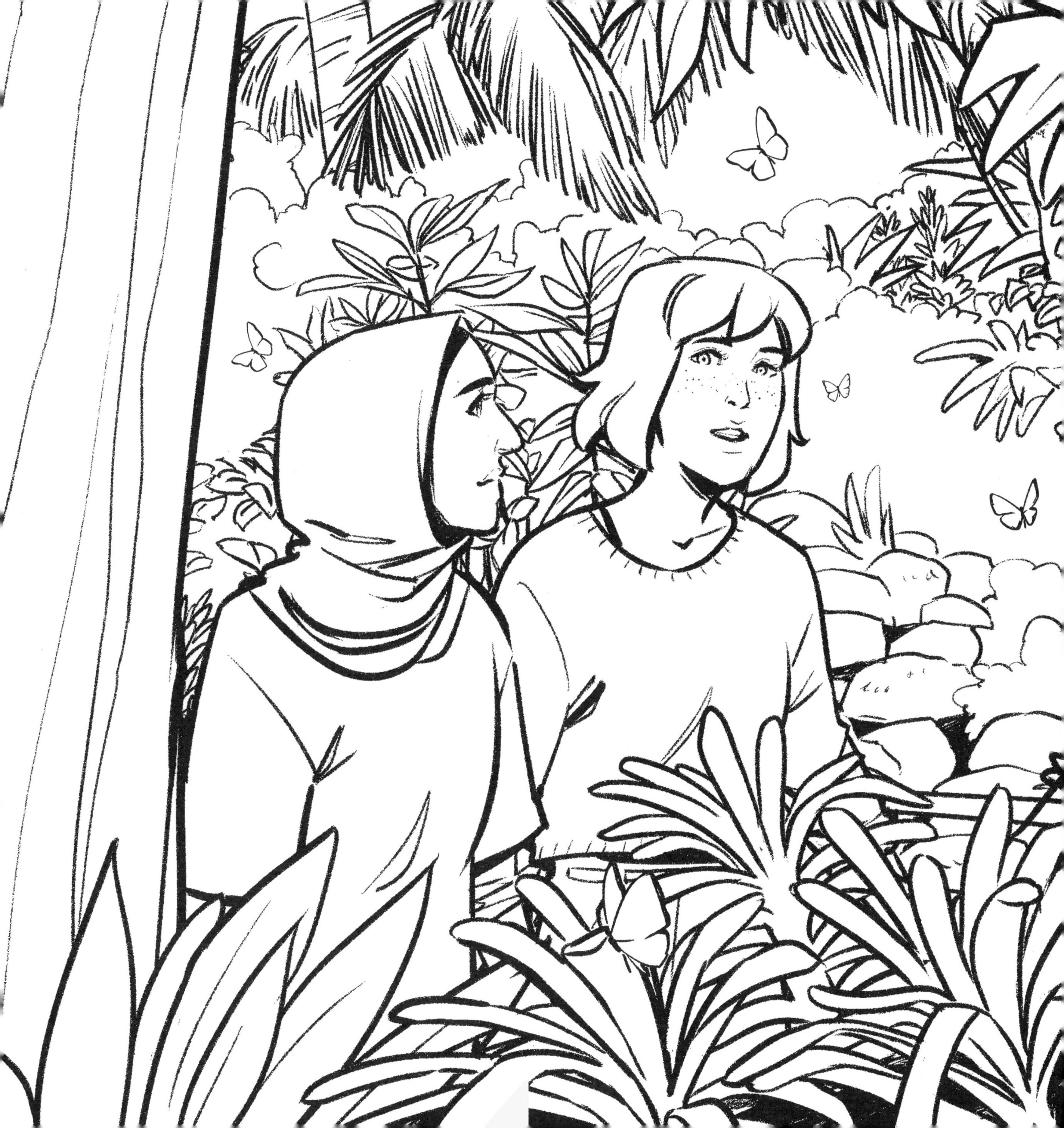

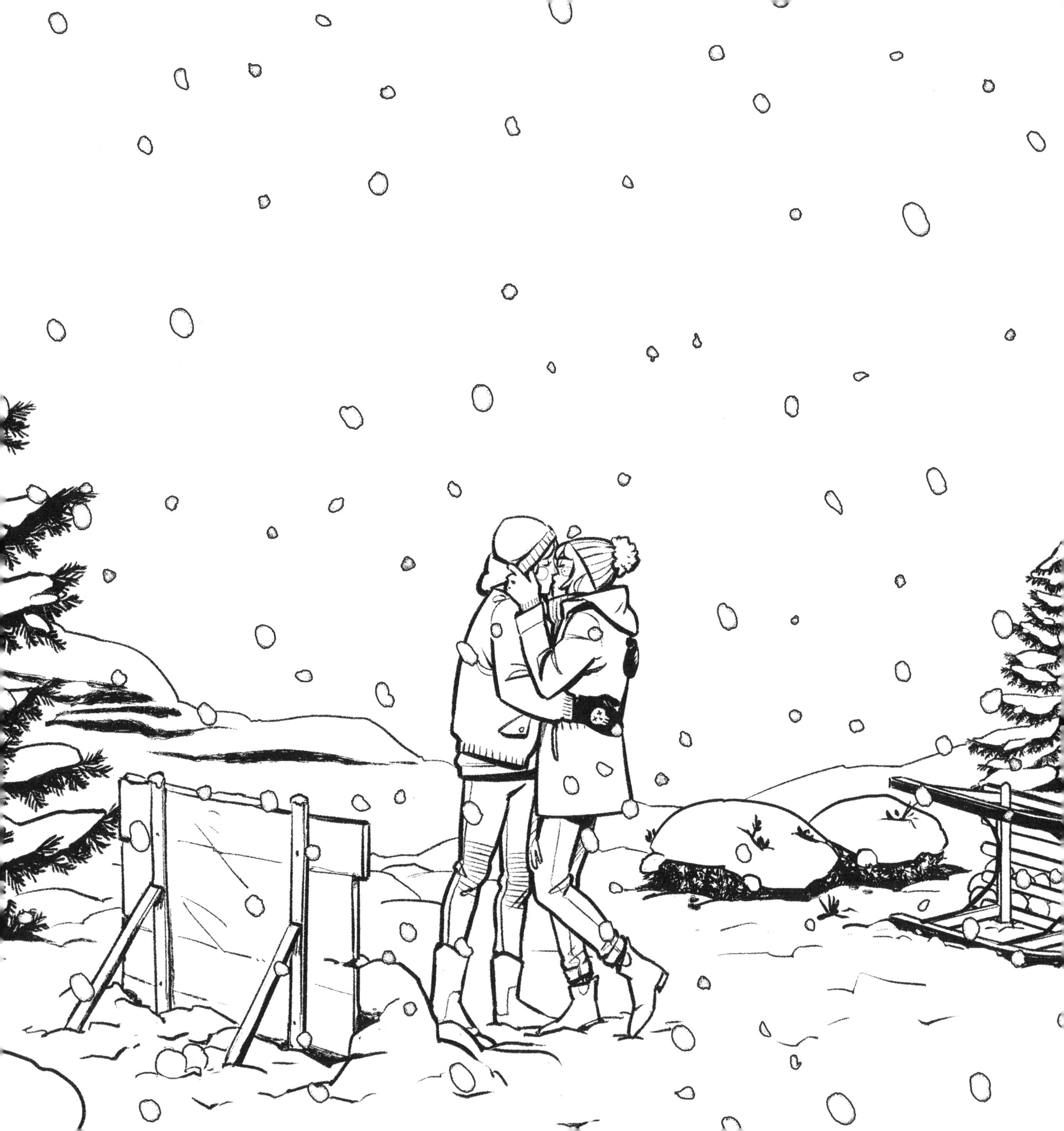

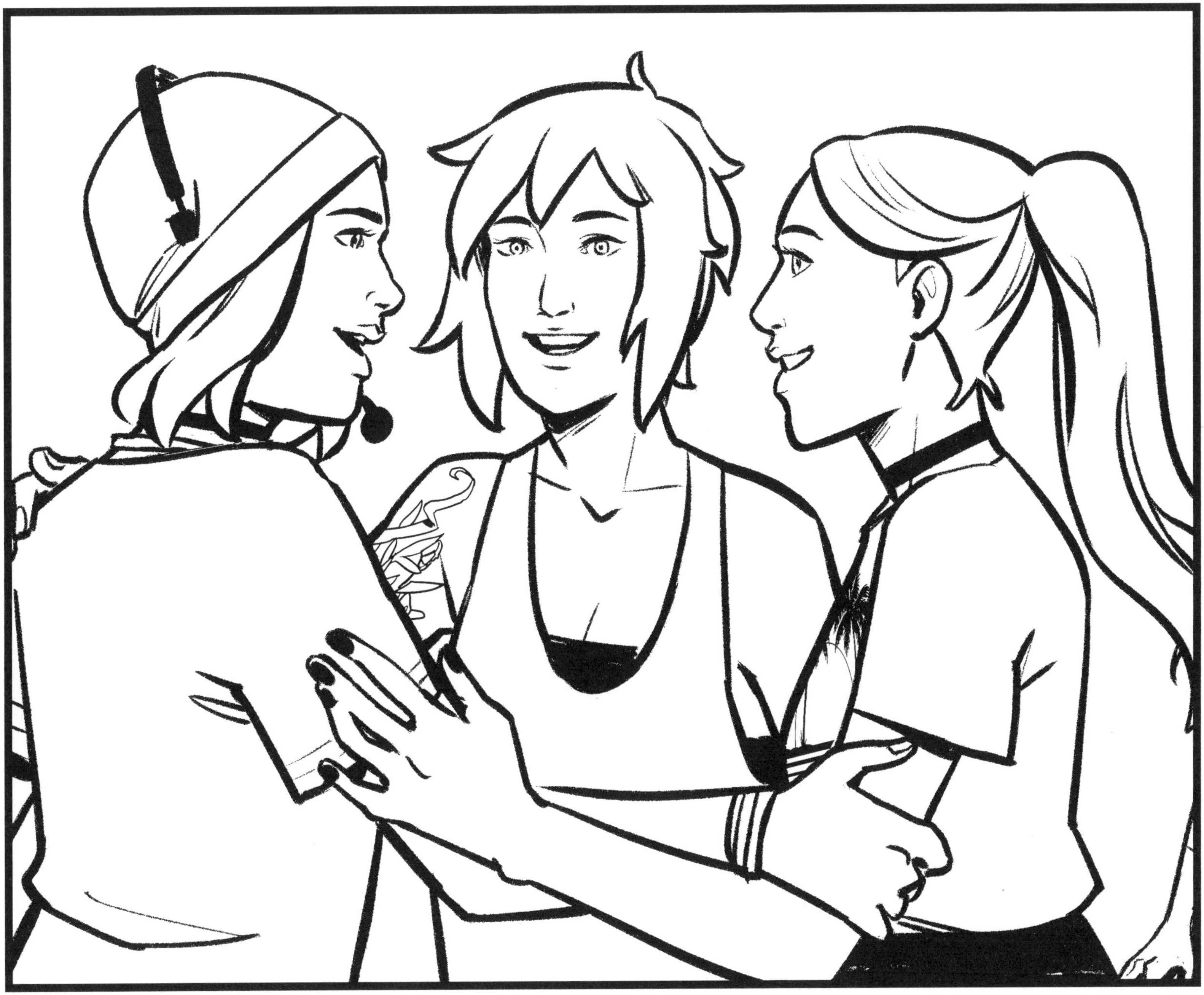

I WOULD NOT WISH ANY COMPANION
IN THE WORLD BUT YOU

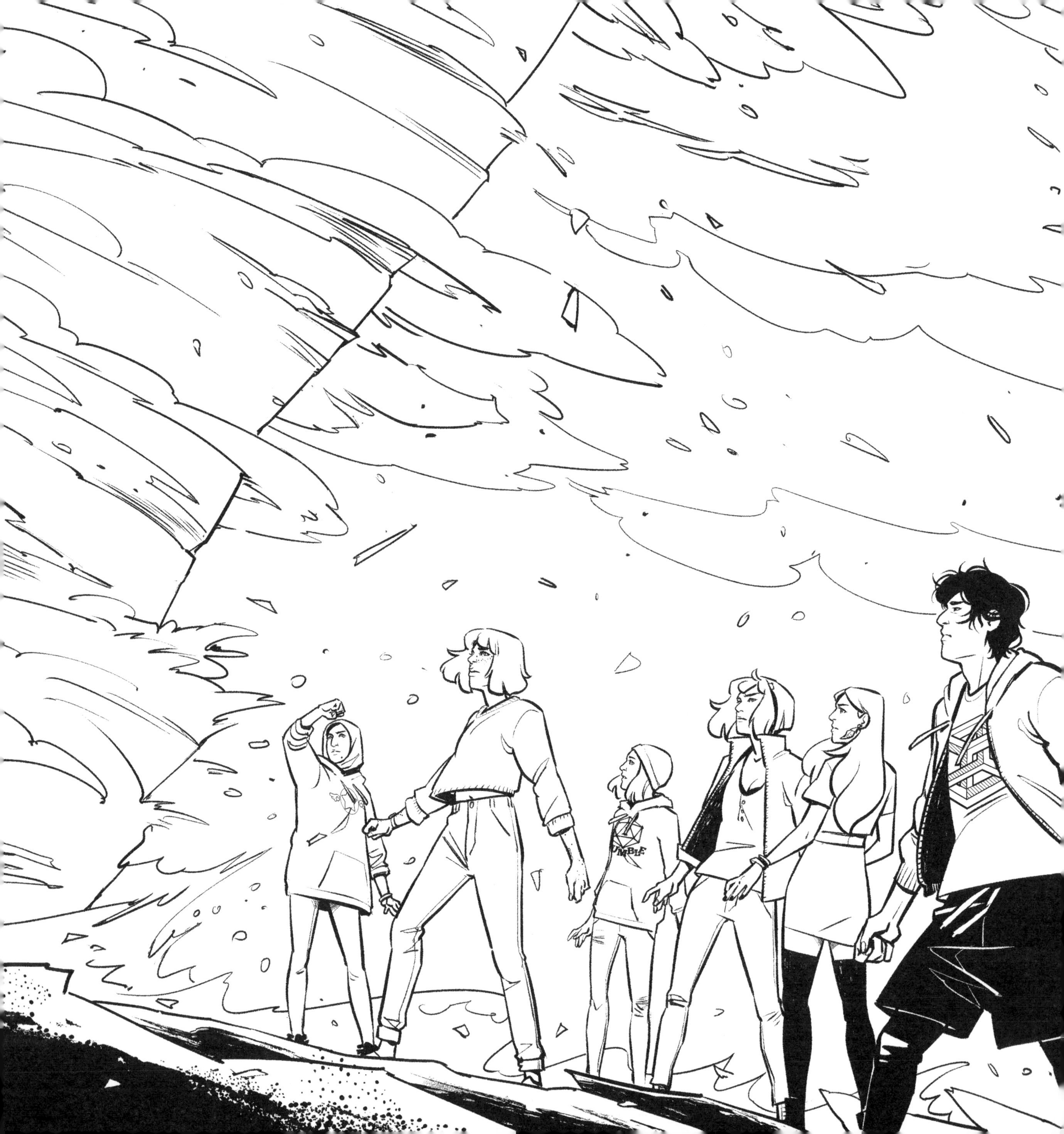

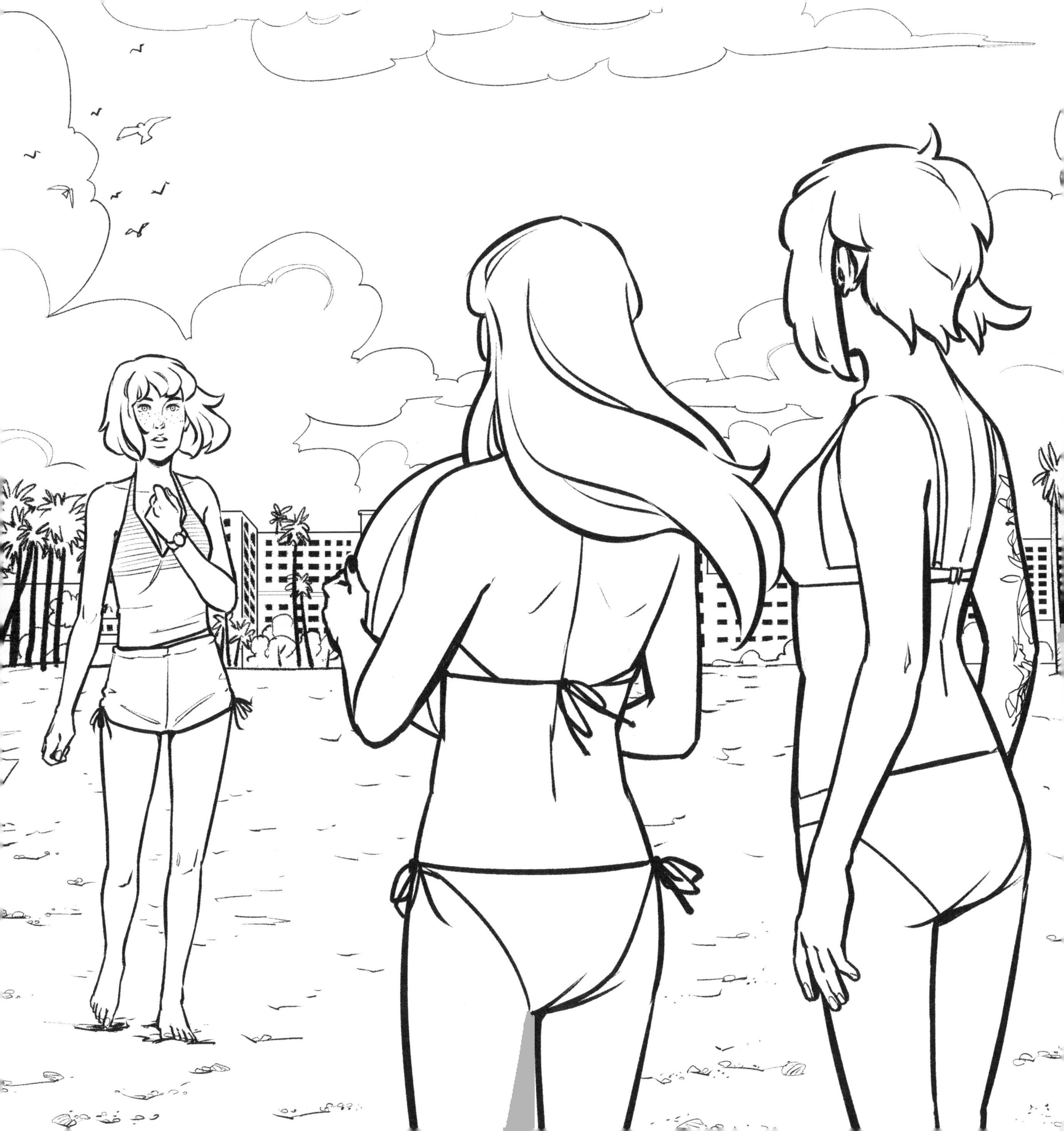

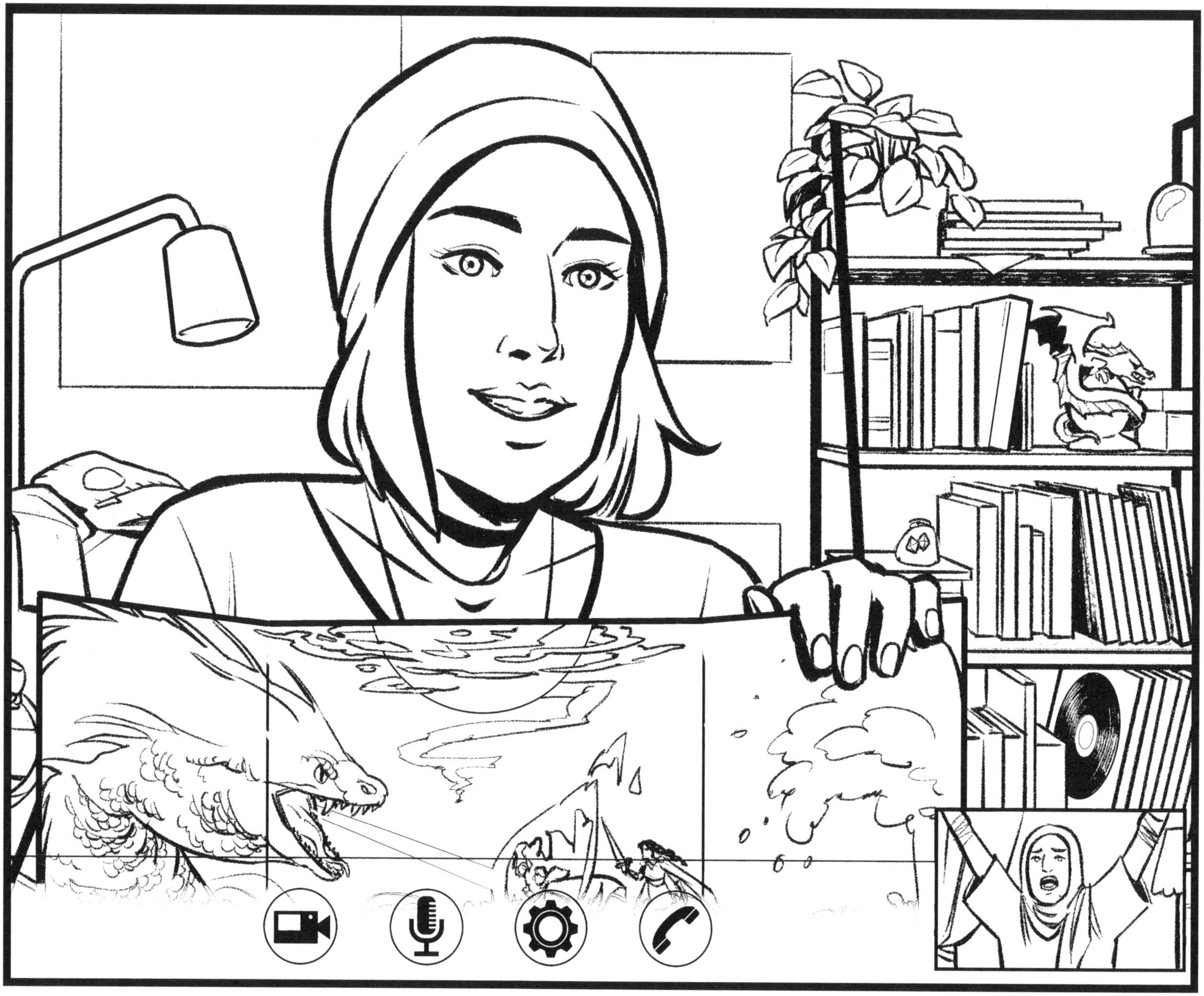

CHOOSE YOUR WEAPON

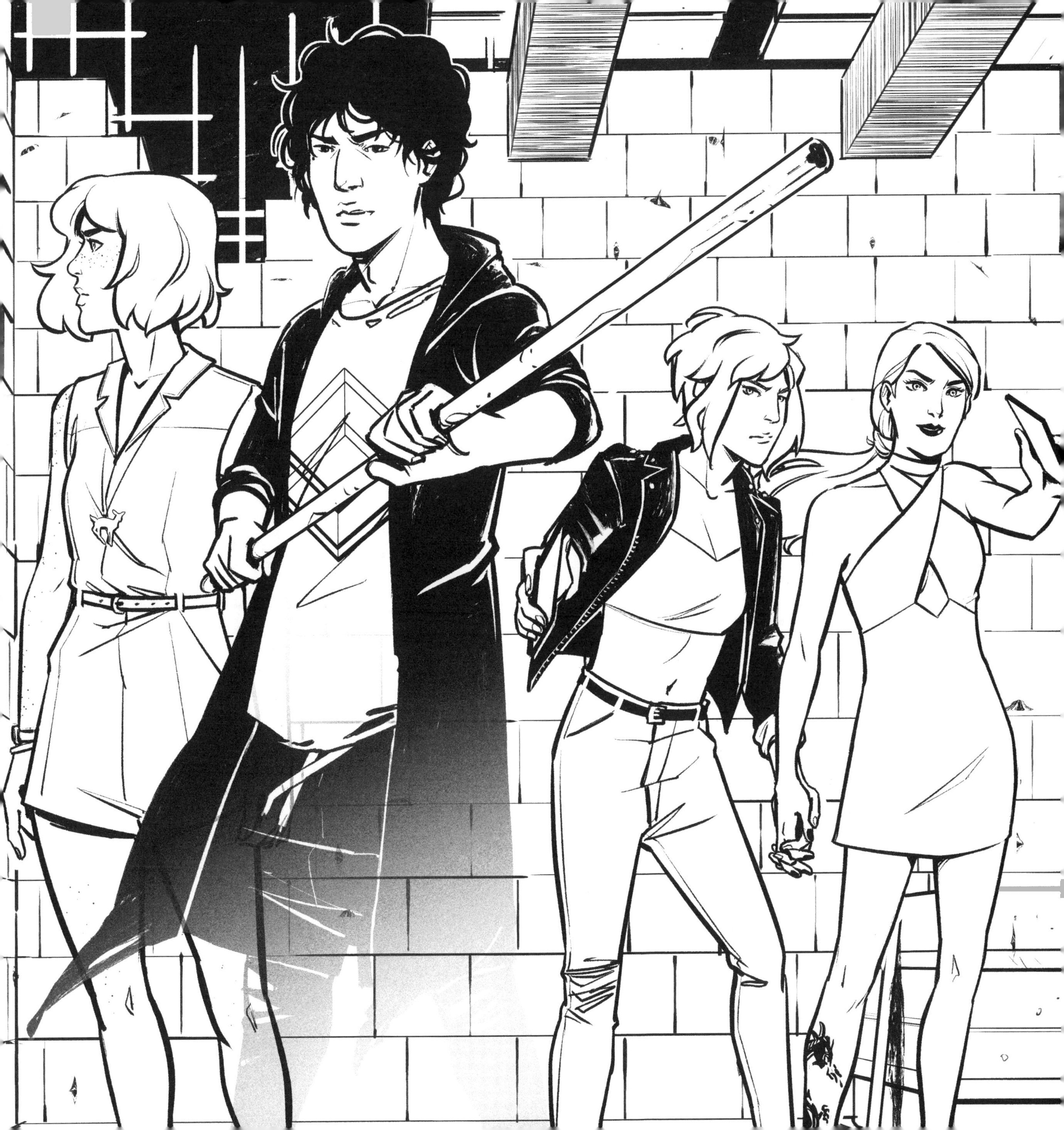

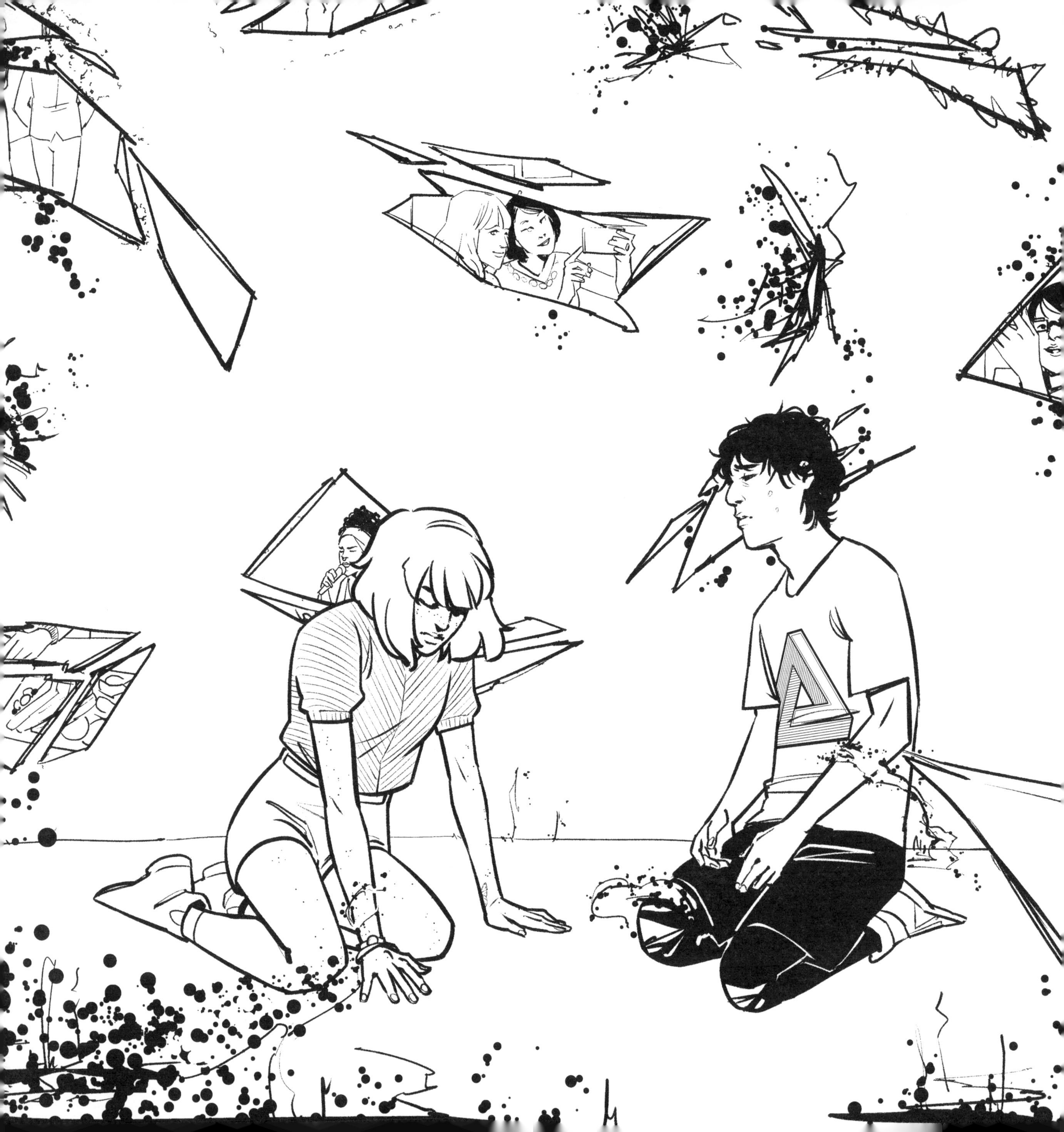

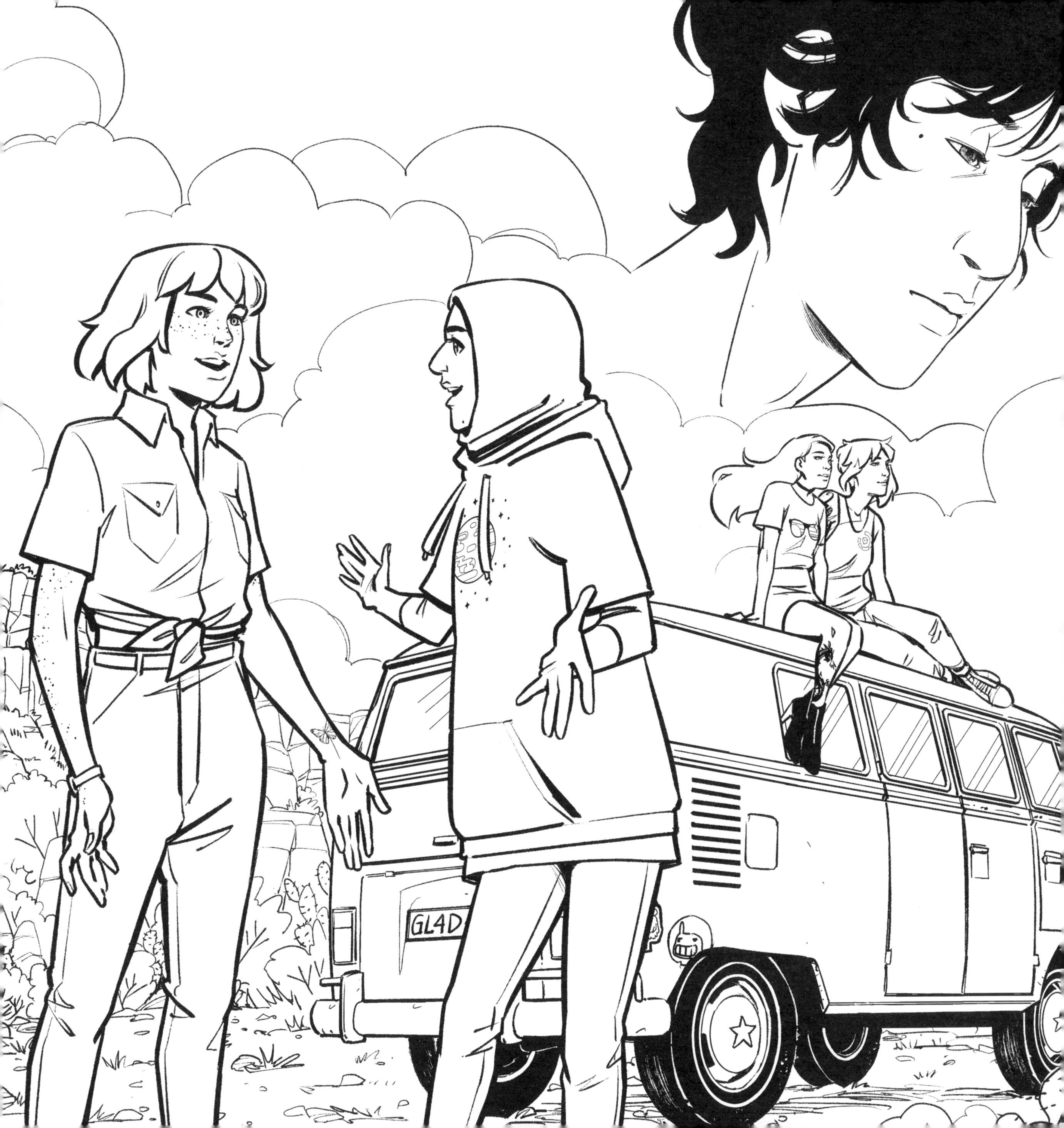
GL4D

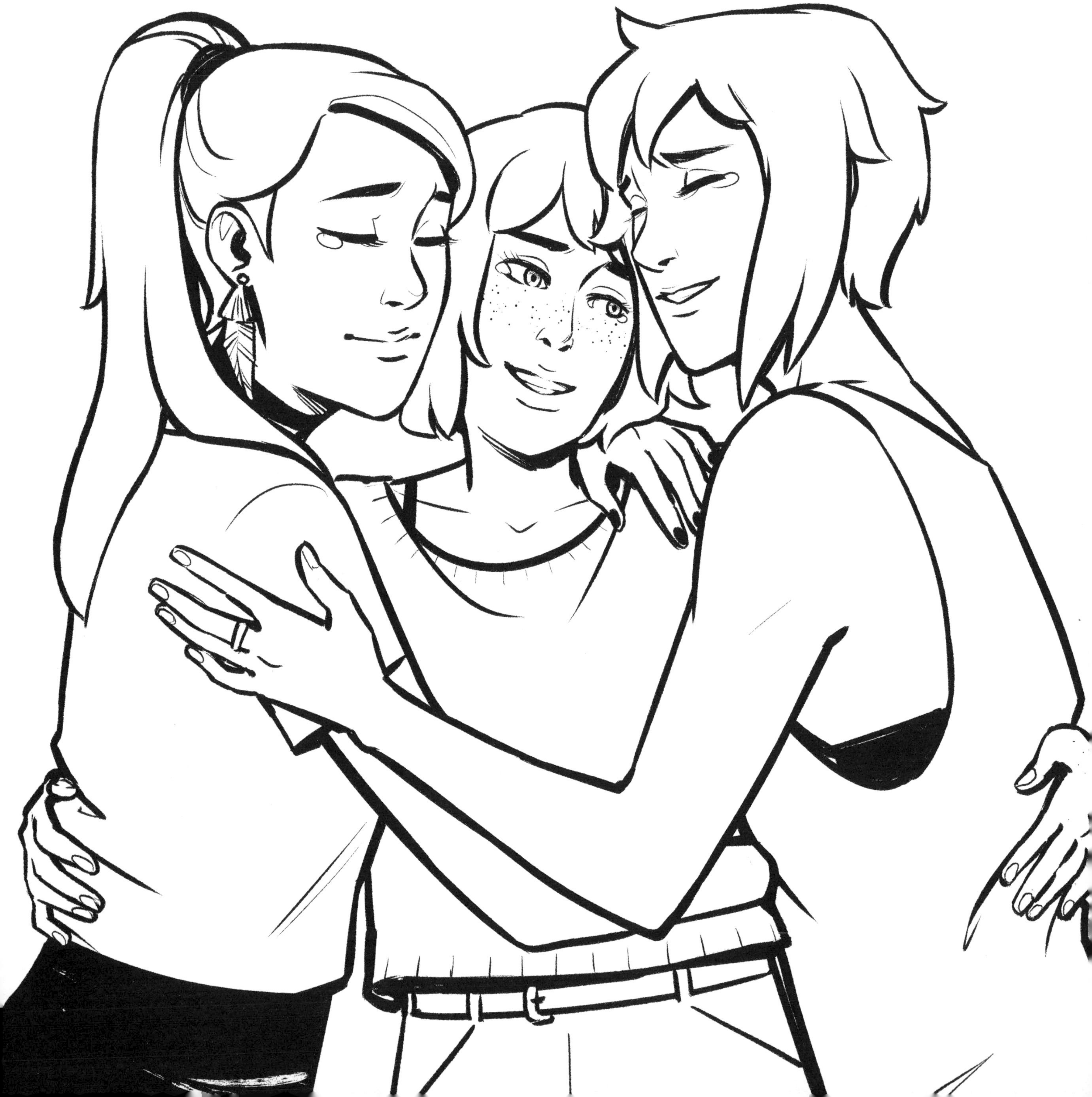

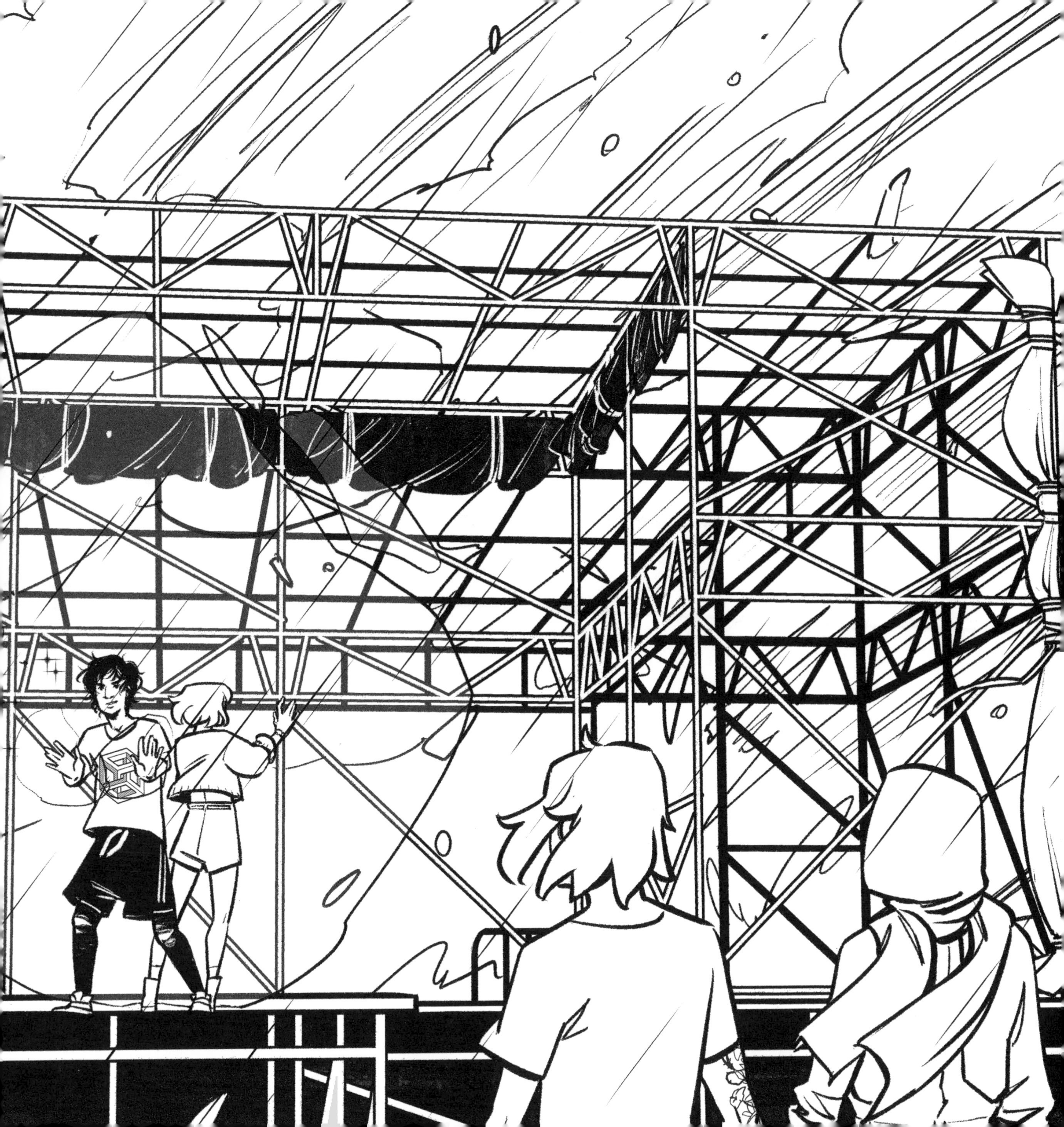

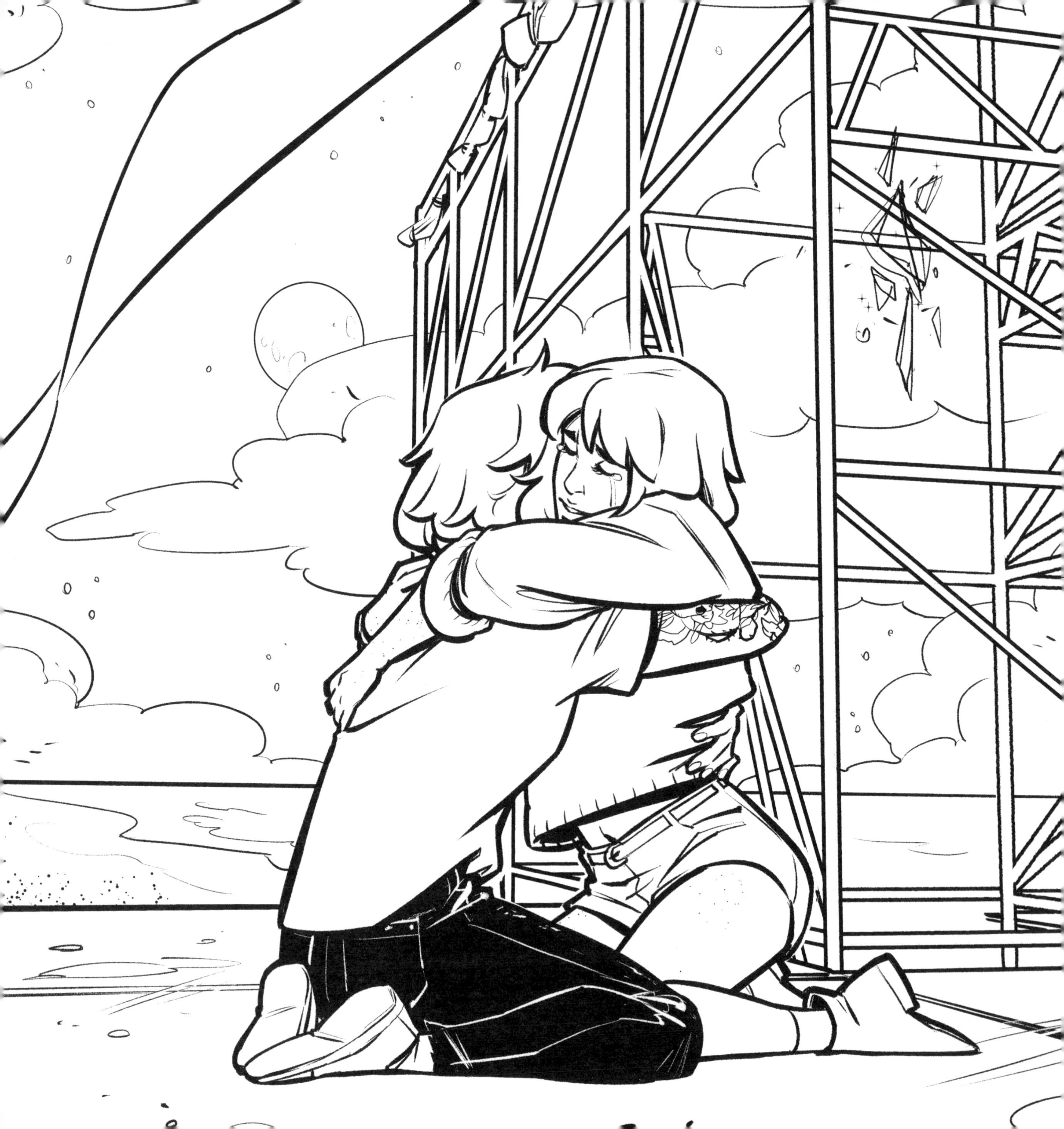

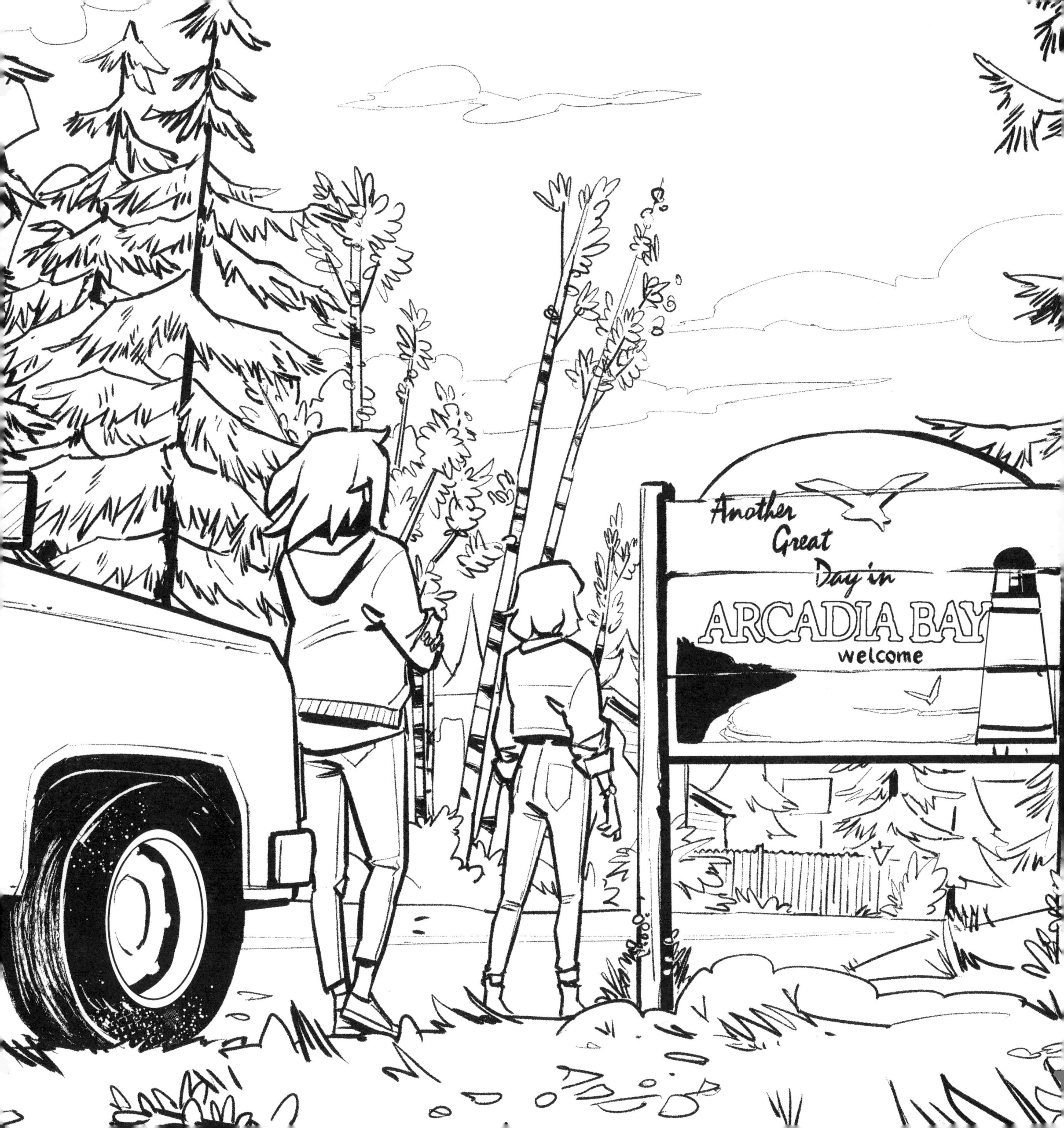
Another Great Day in
ARCADIA BAY
welcome

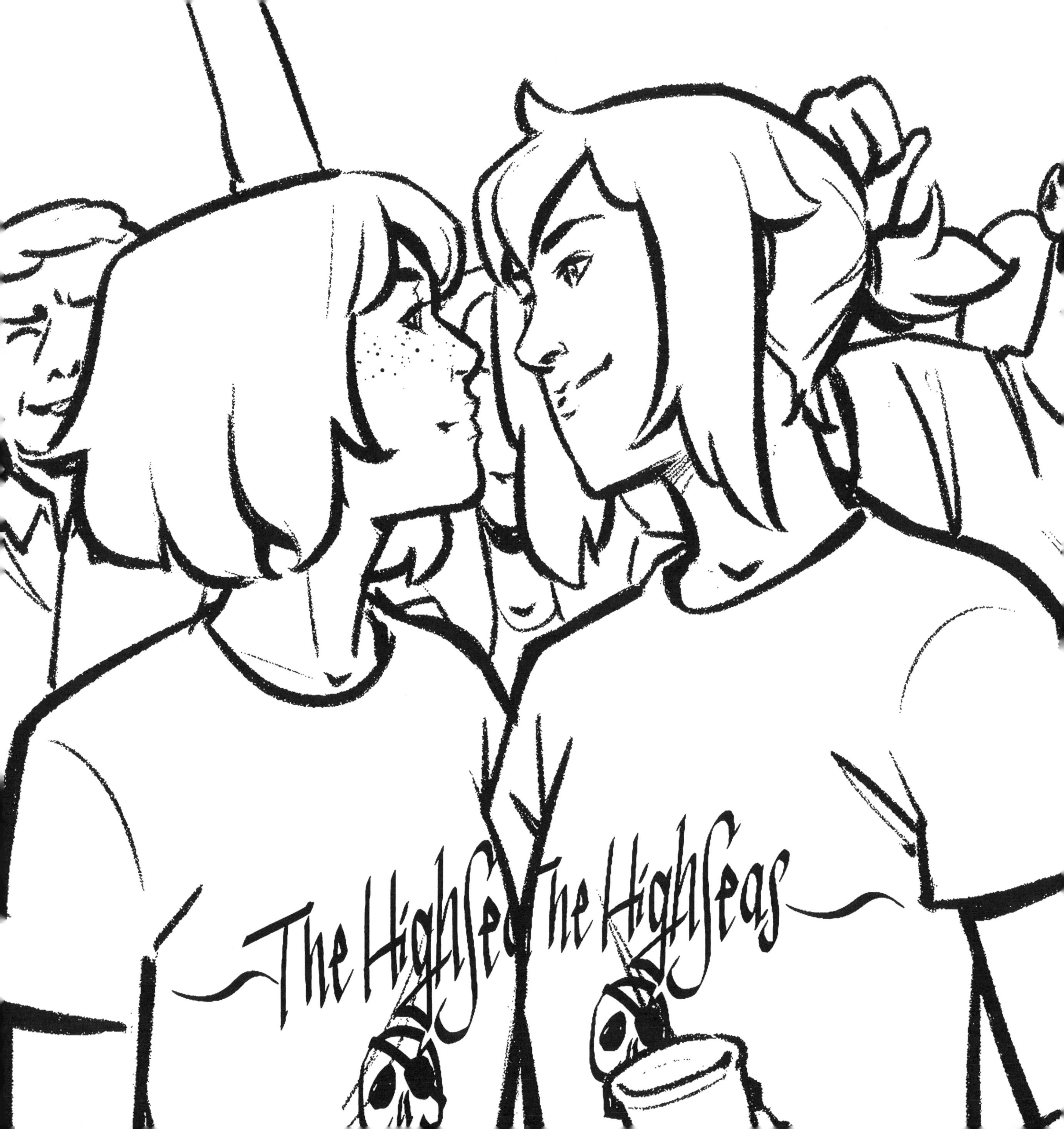
The High Sea
he High Seas

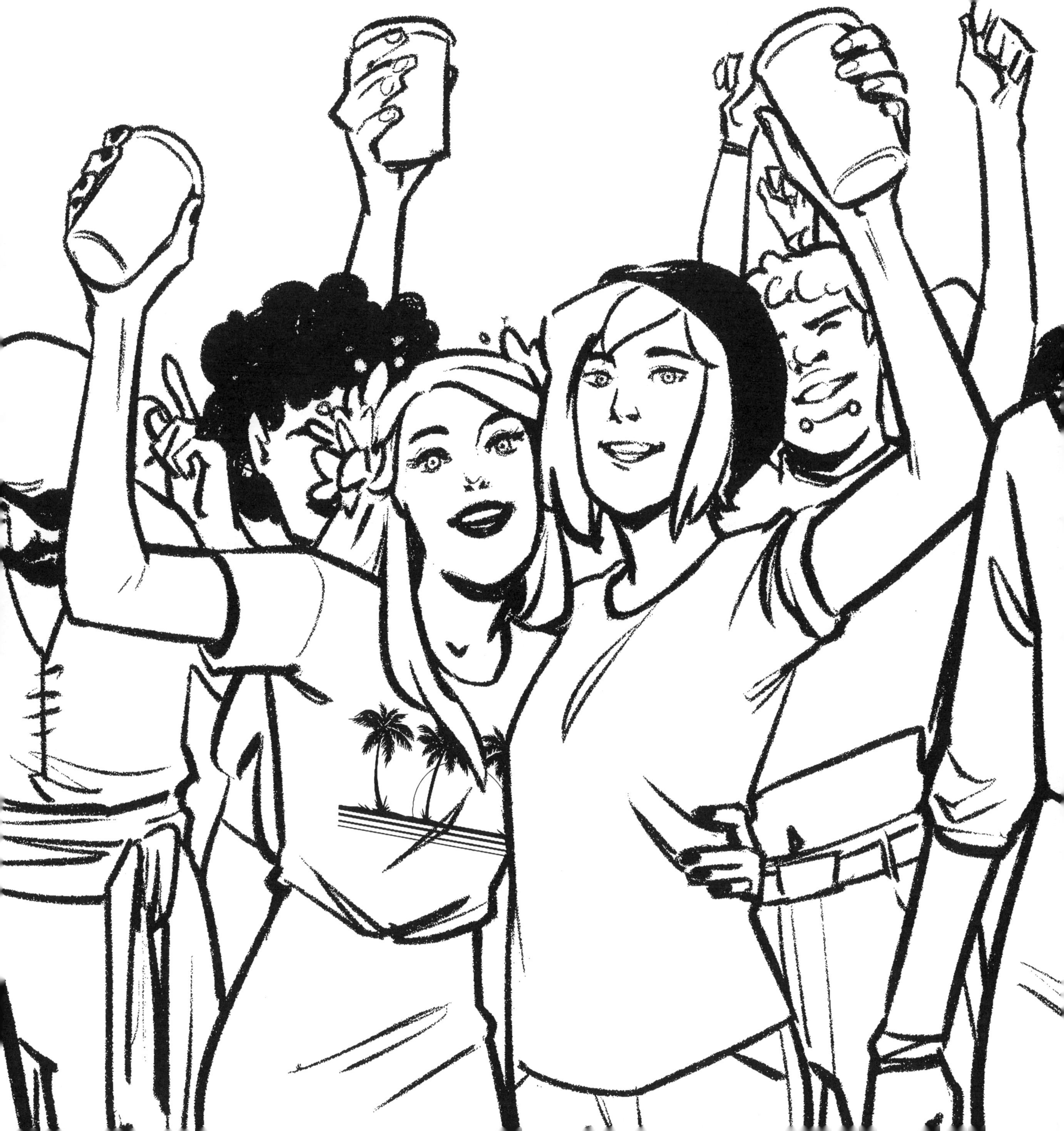

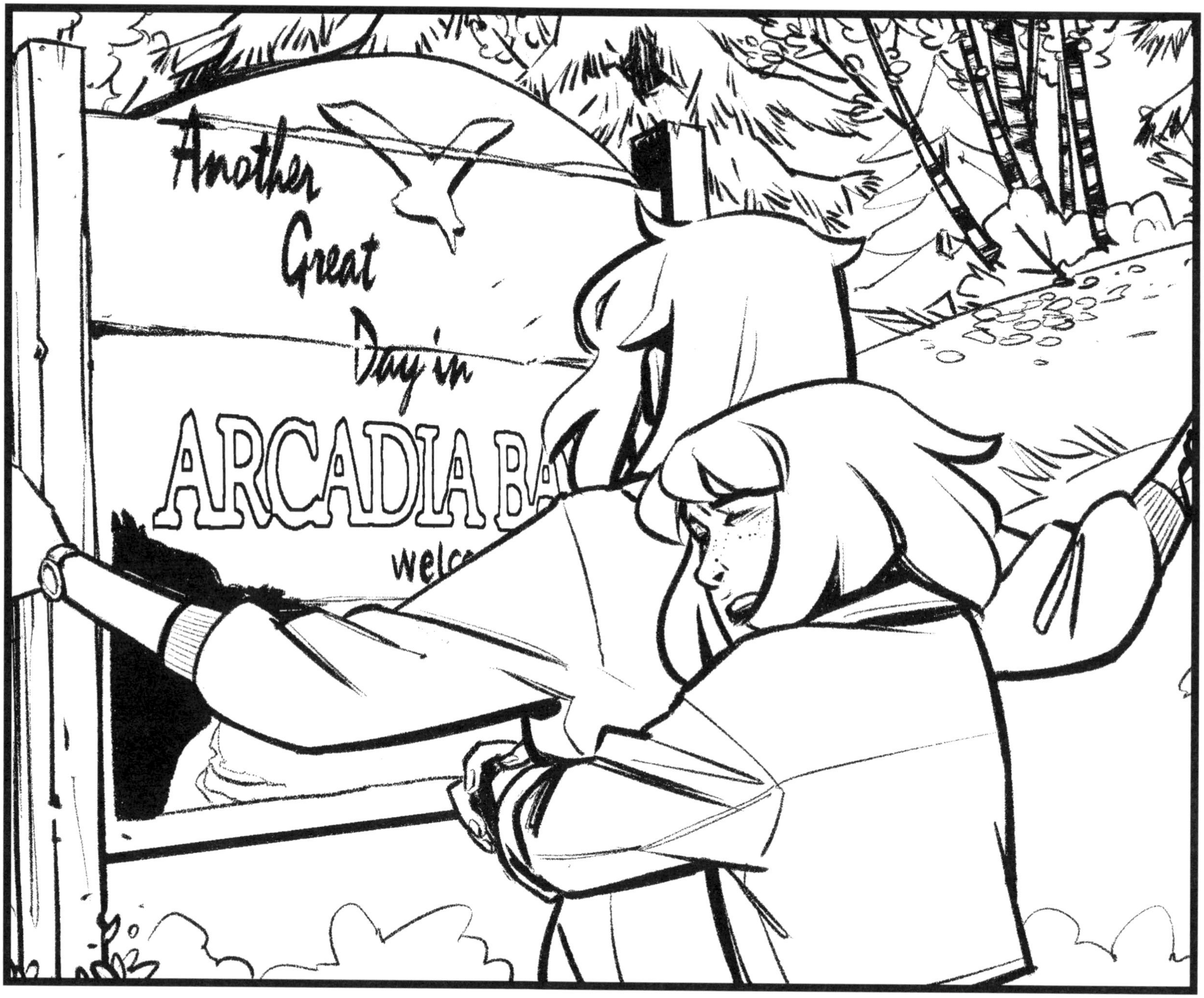
Another Great Day in
ARCADIA BA
welc

NO MORE LIES

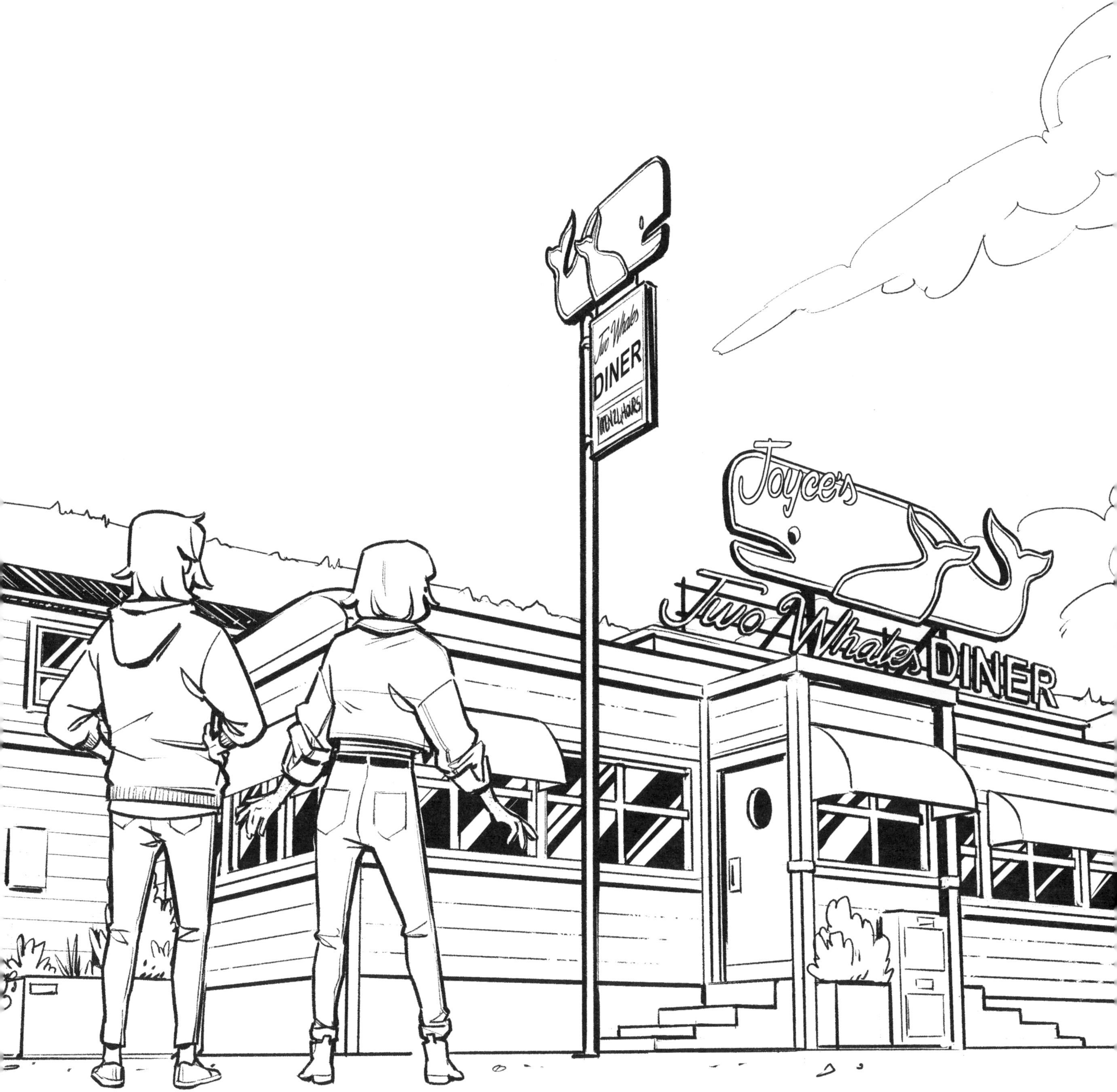
Two Whales
DINER
OPEN 24 HOURS
Joyce's
Two Whales DINER

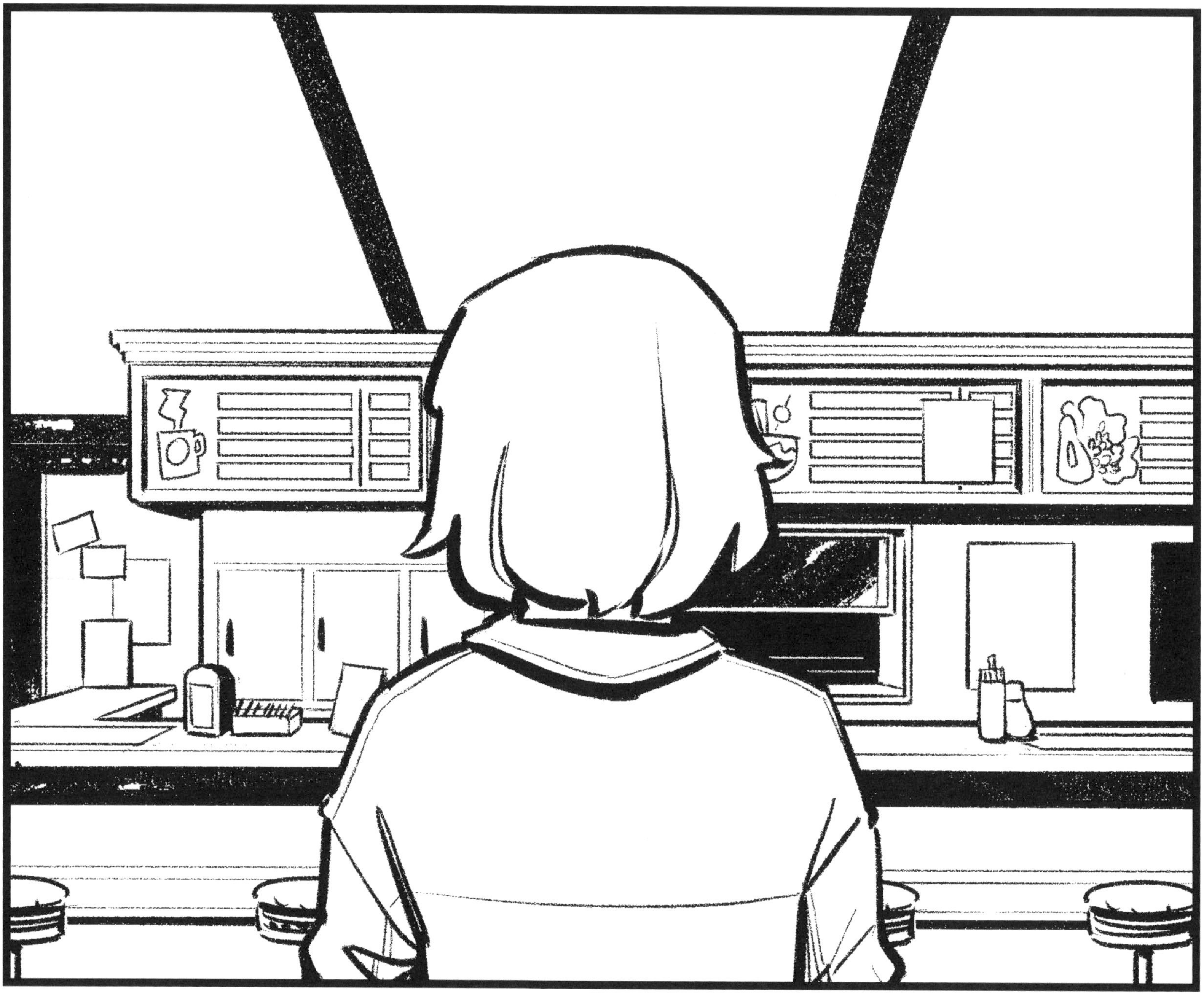

WOAH, MAJOR DEJA VU

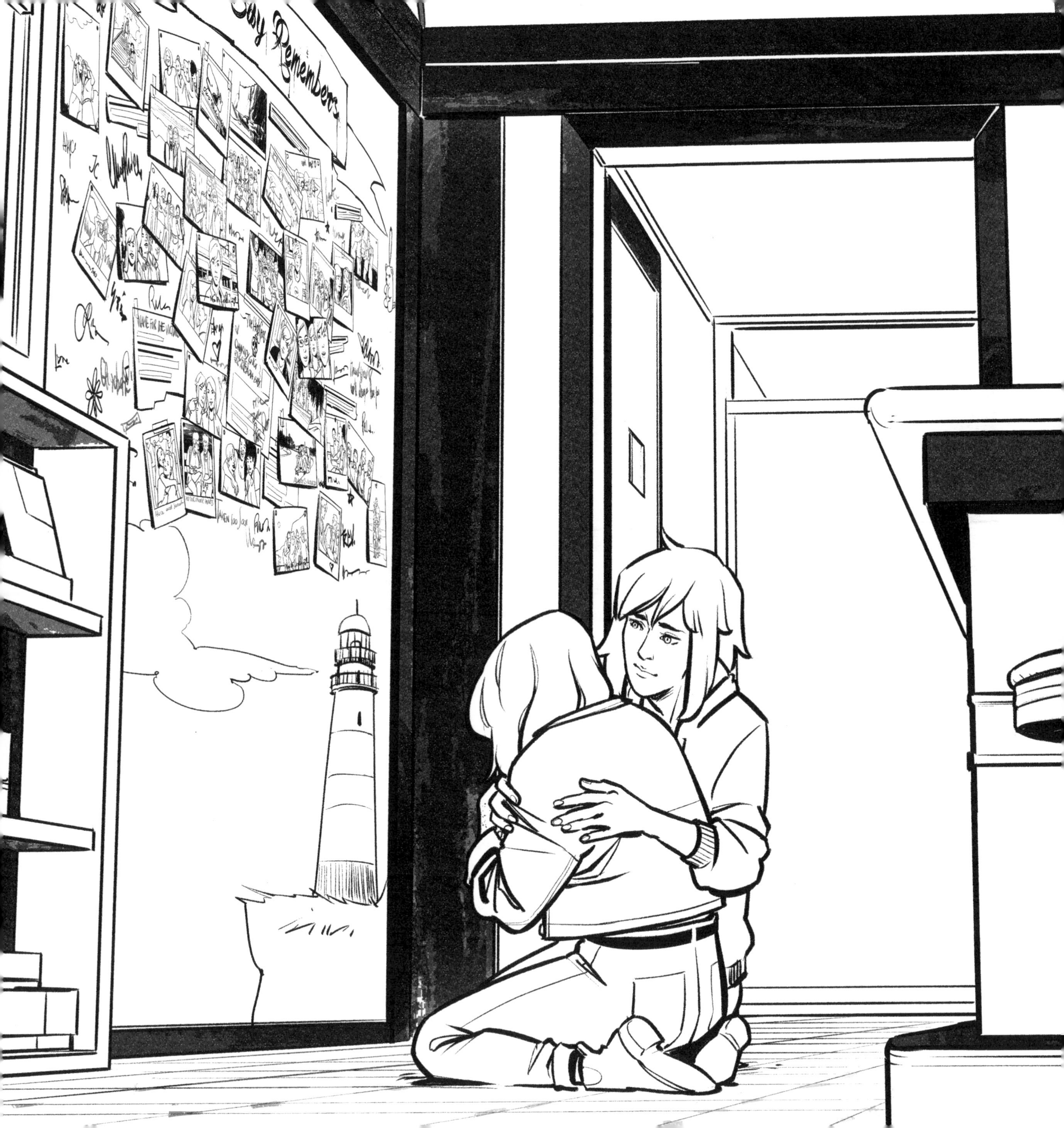
Remembers

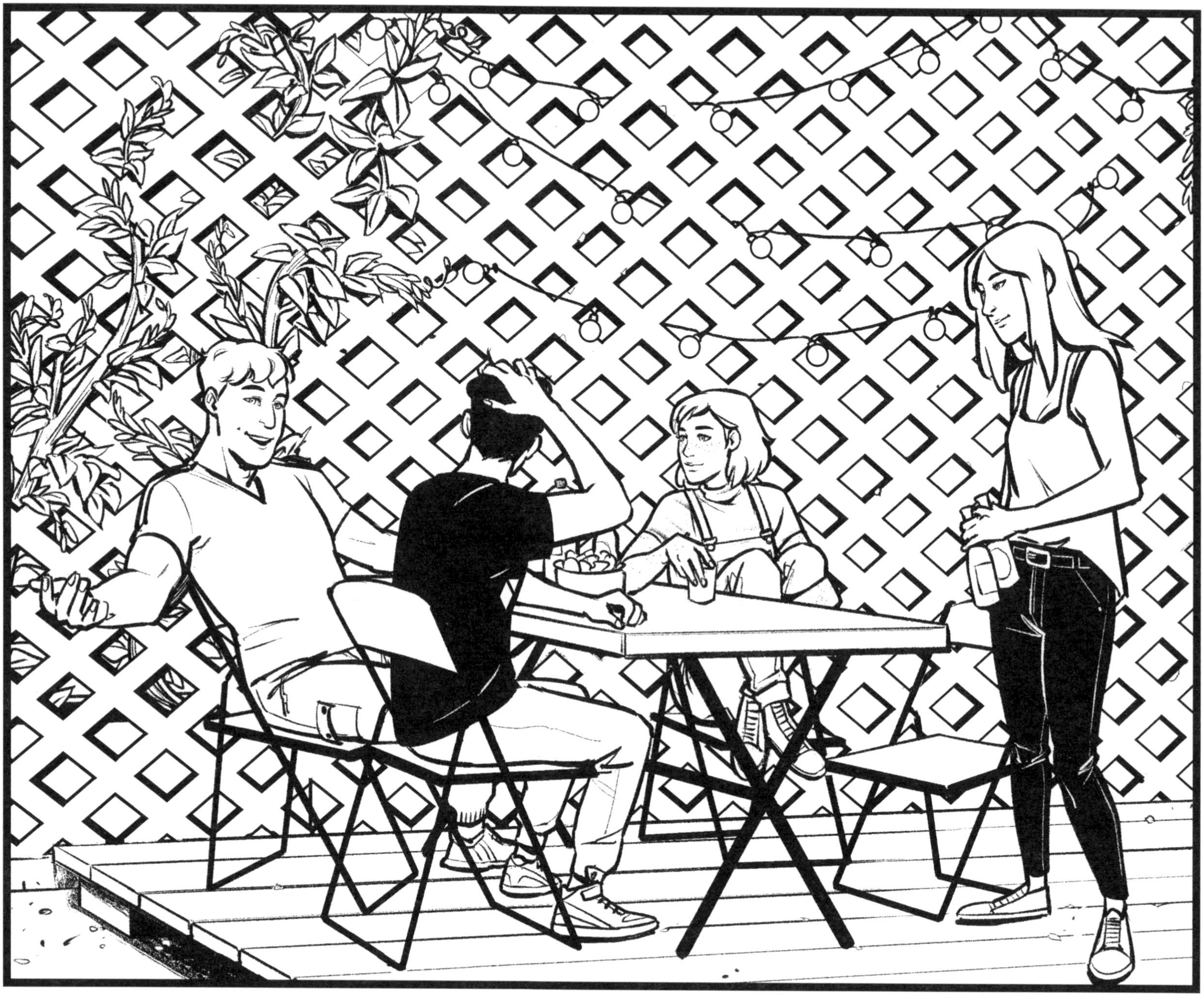

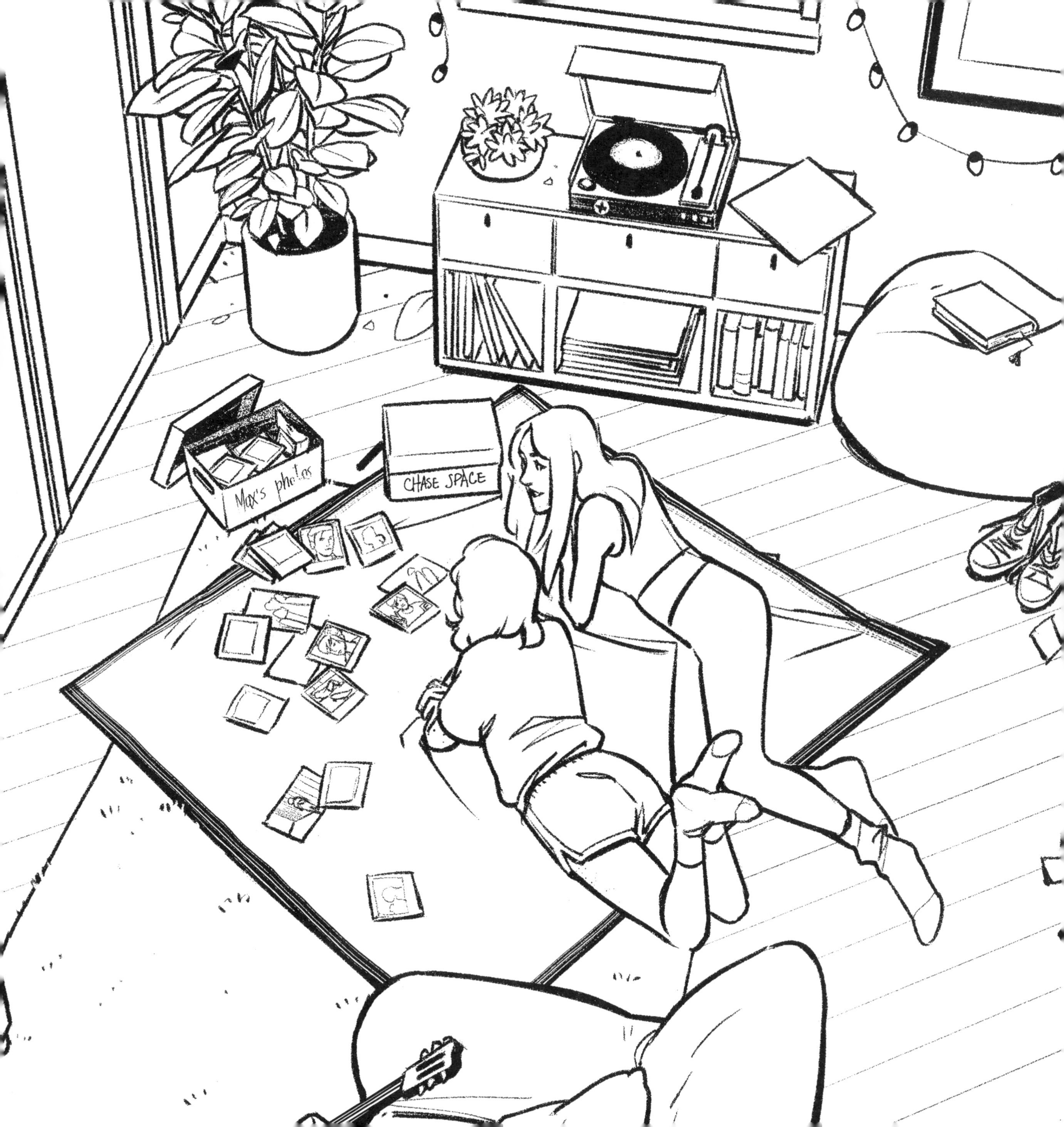
Max's photos
CHASE SPACE

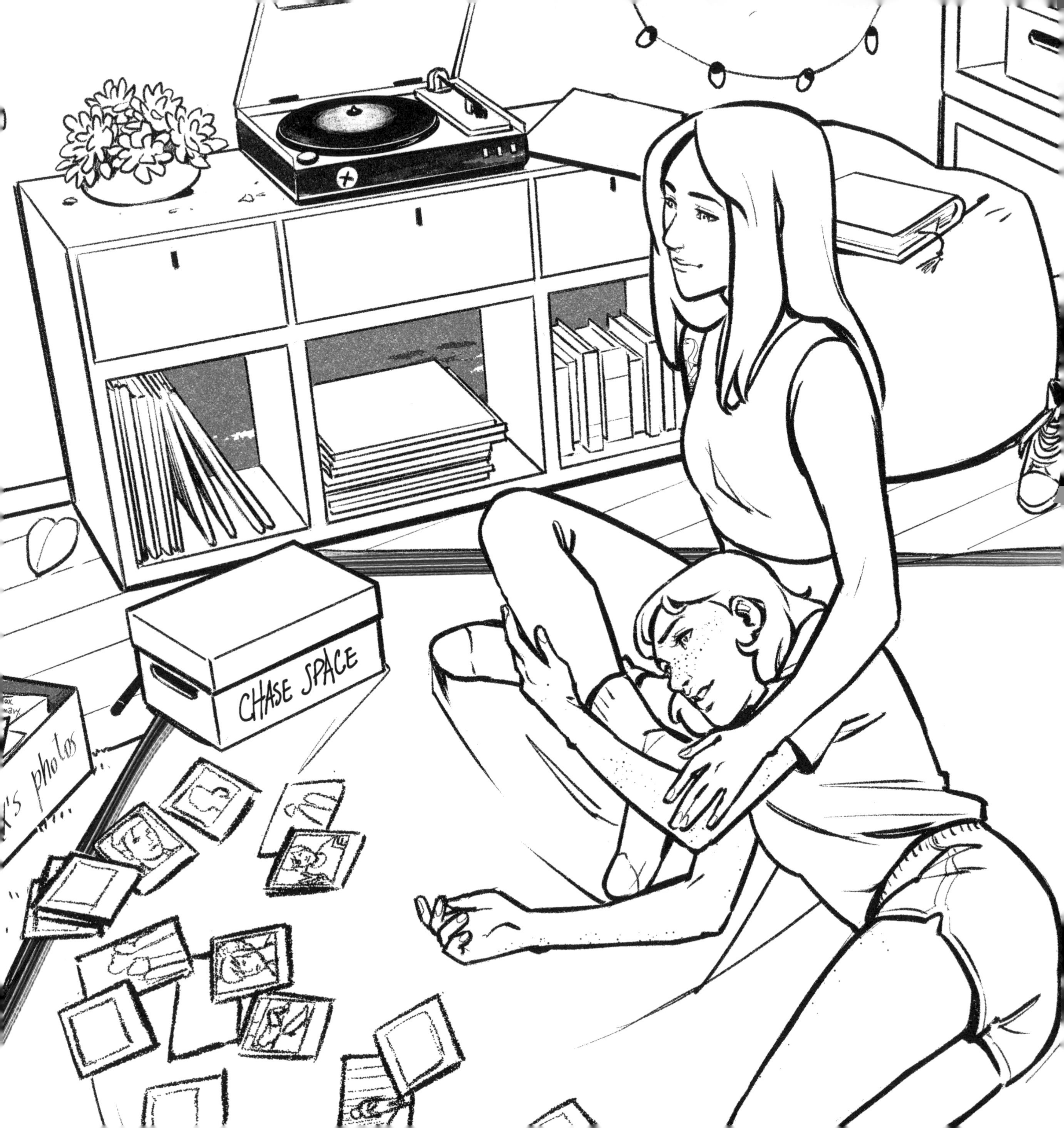
CHASE SPACE

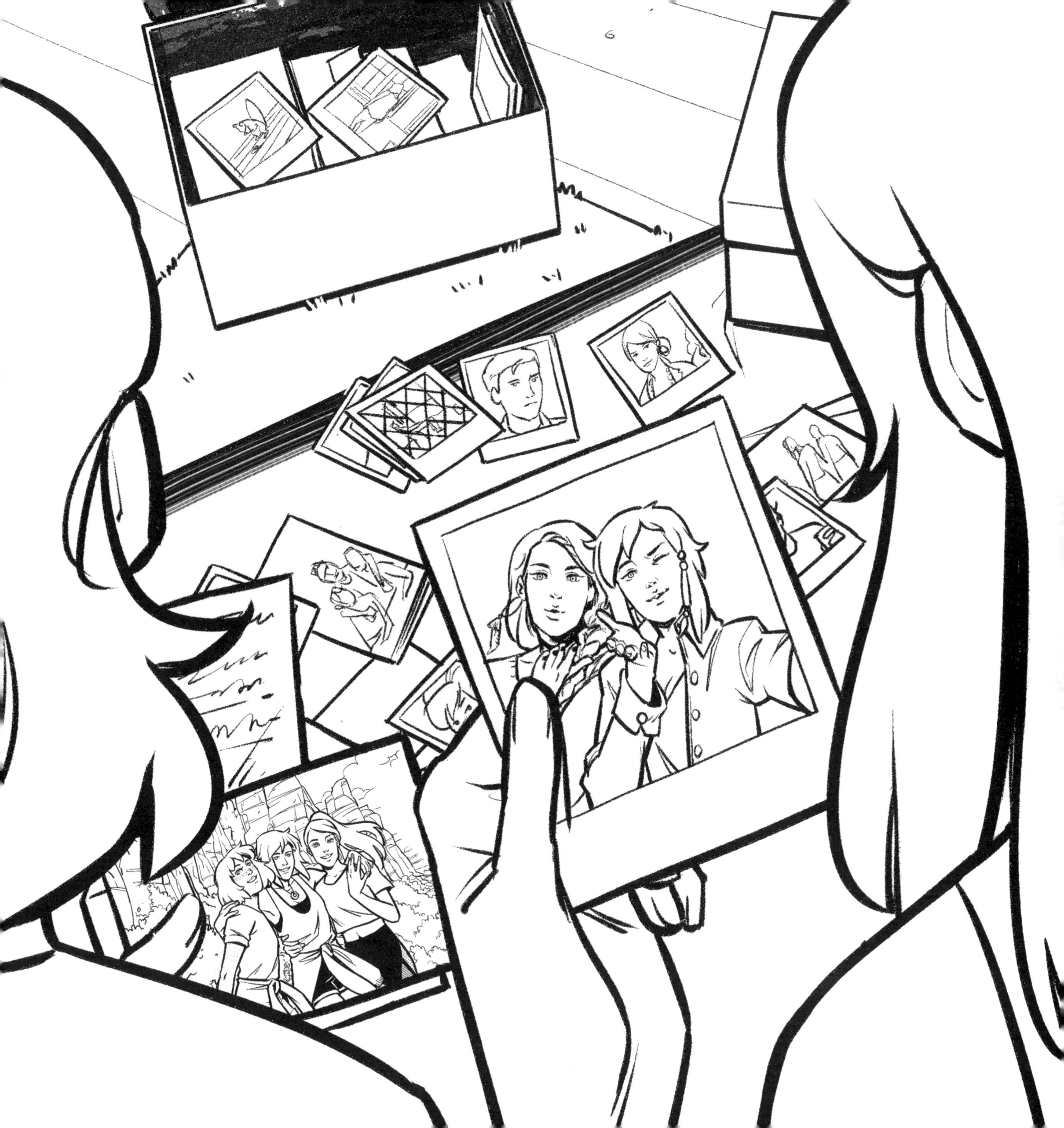

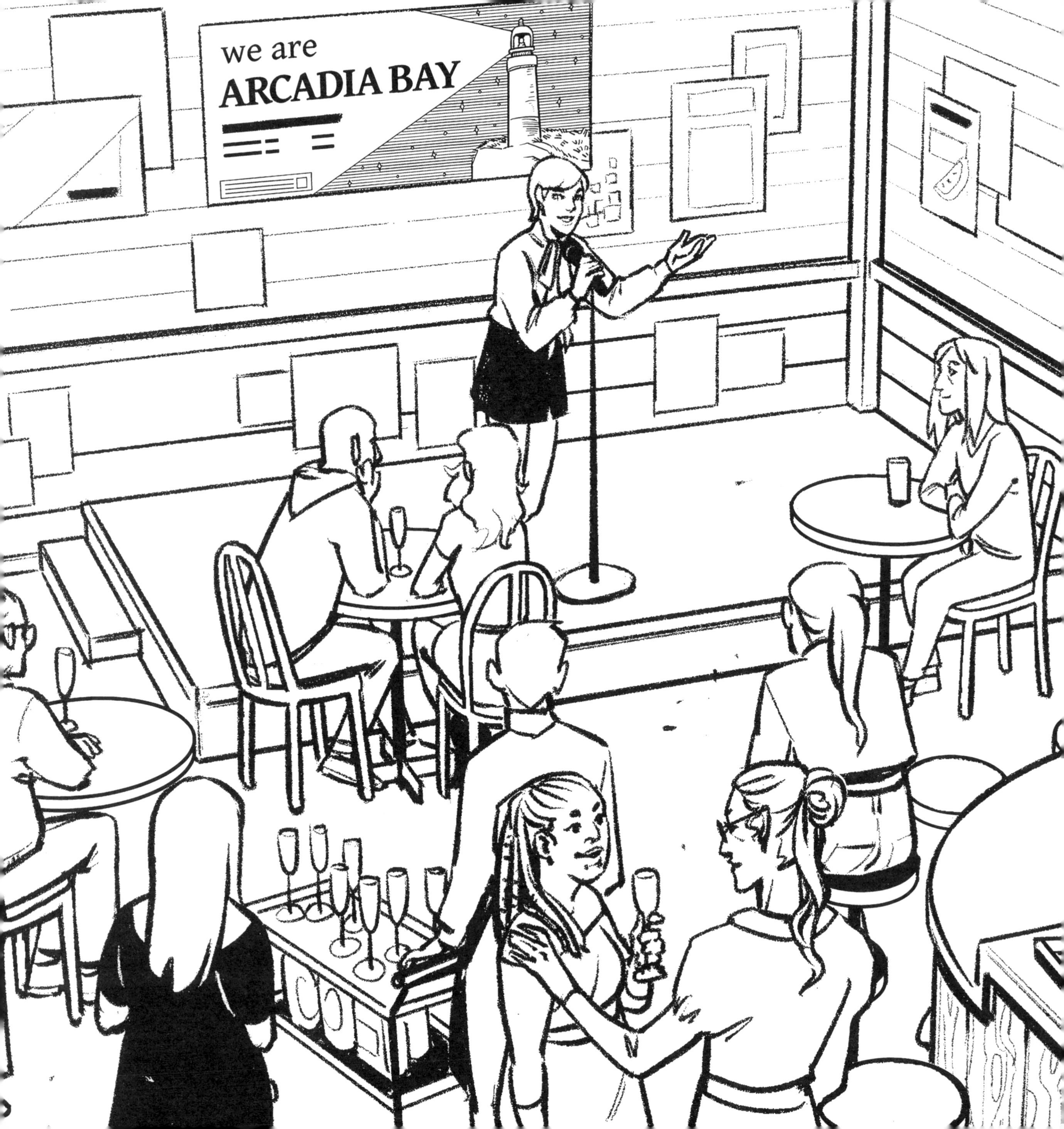
we are
ARCADIA BAY

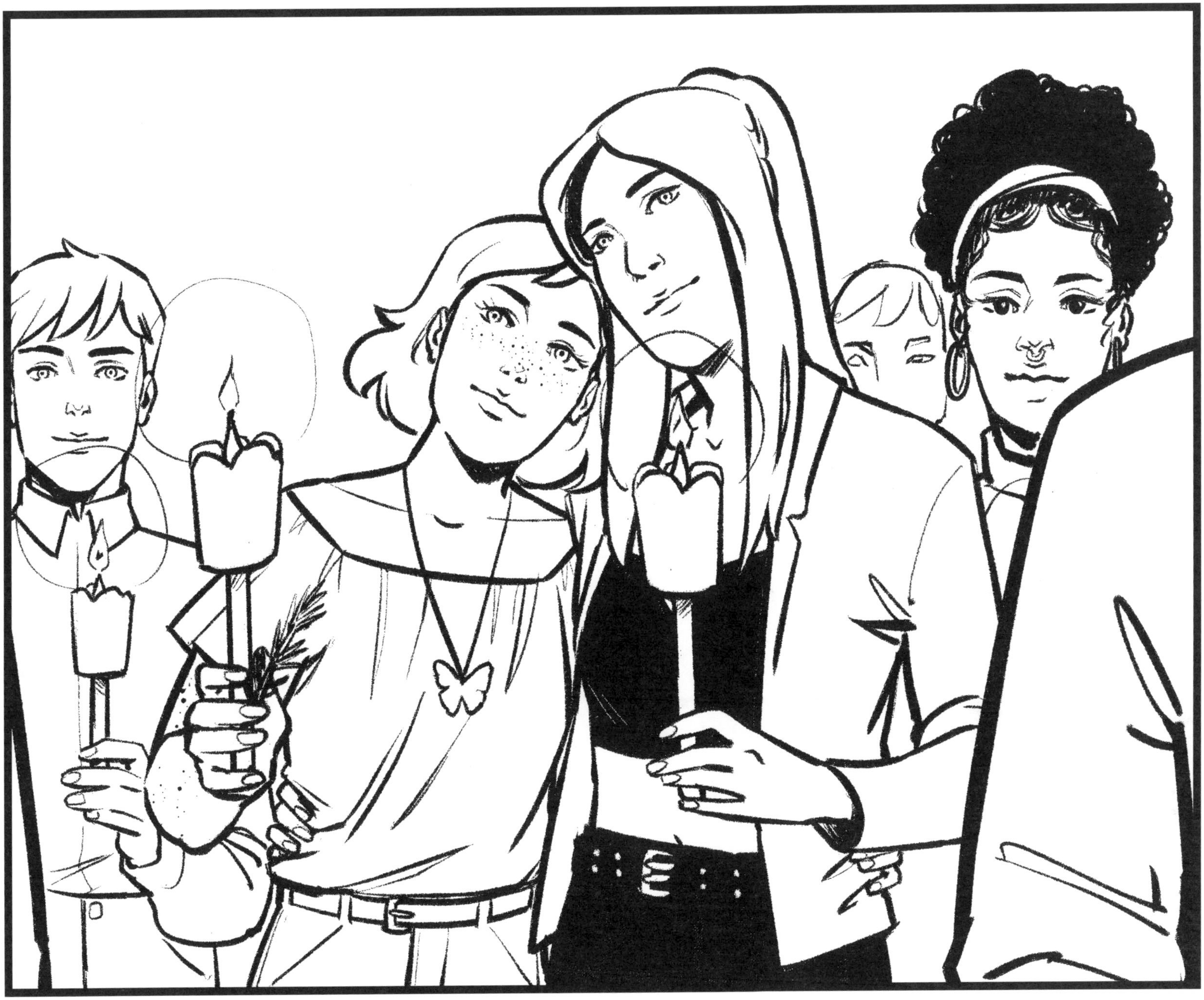

ROSEMARY, FOR REMEMBRANCE

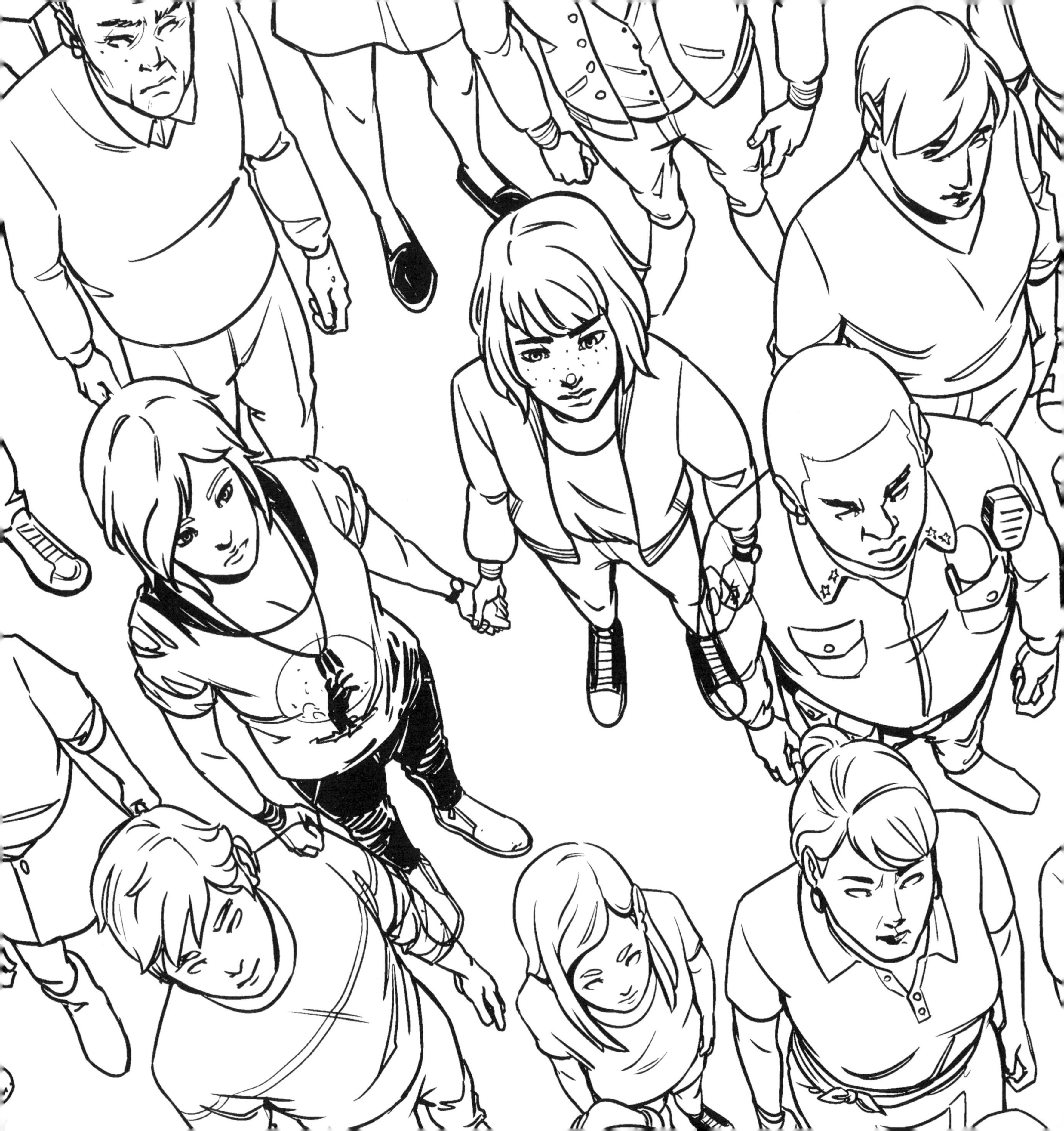

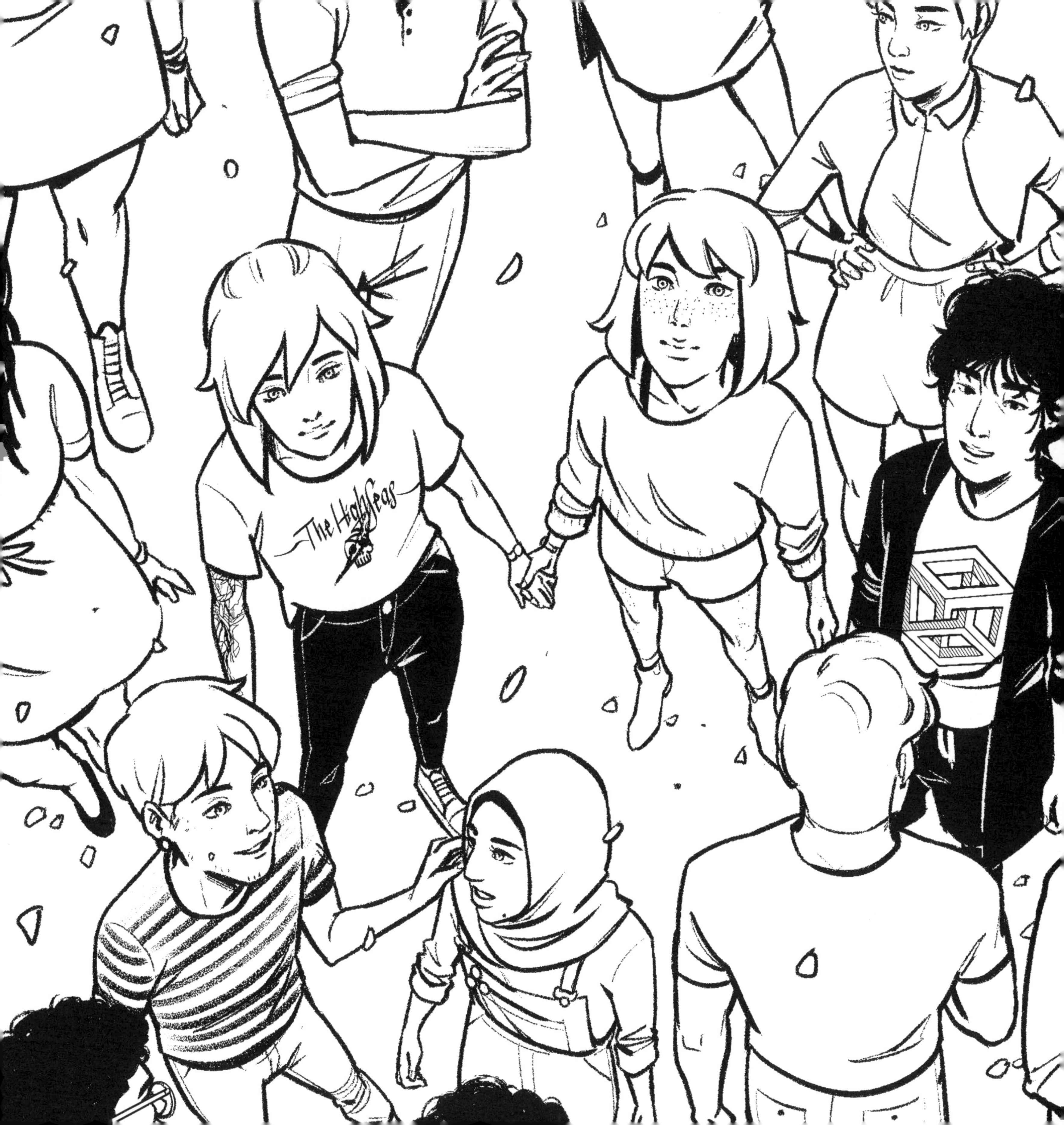
The HighSeas

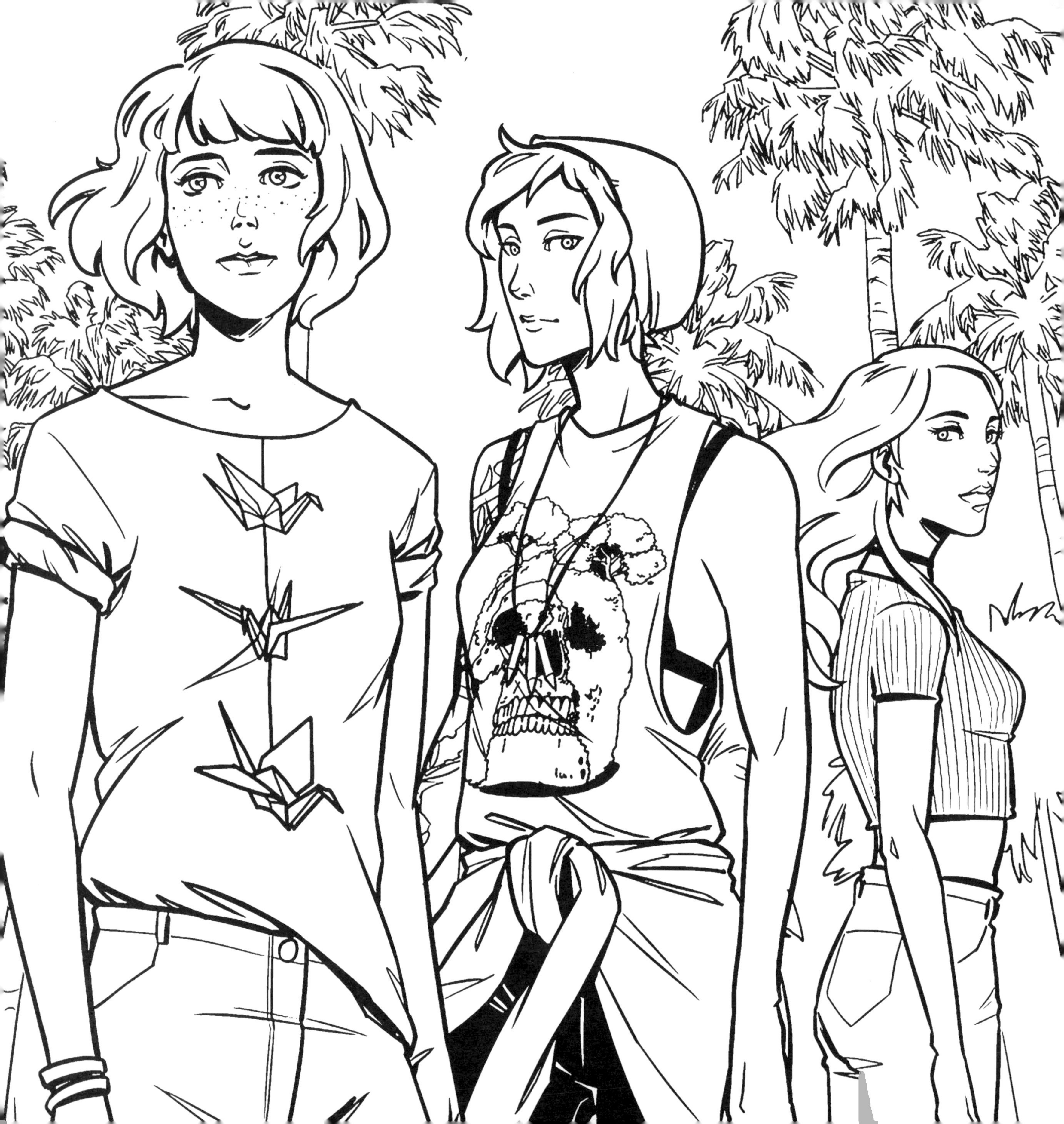

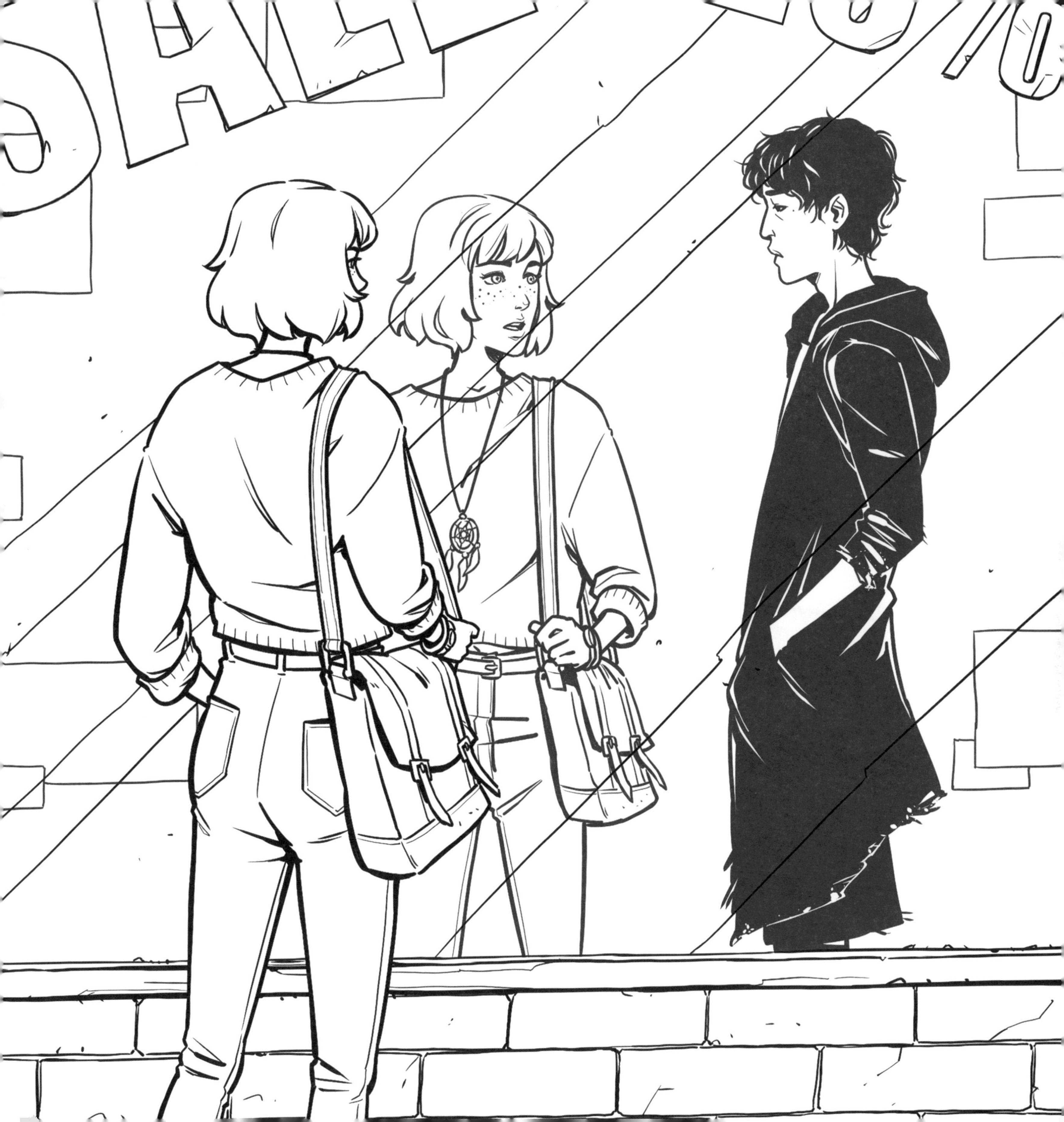

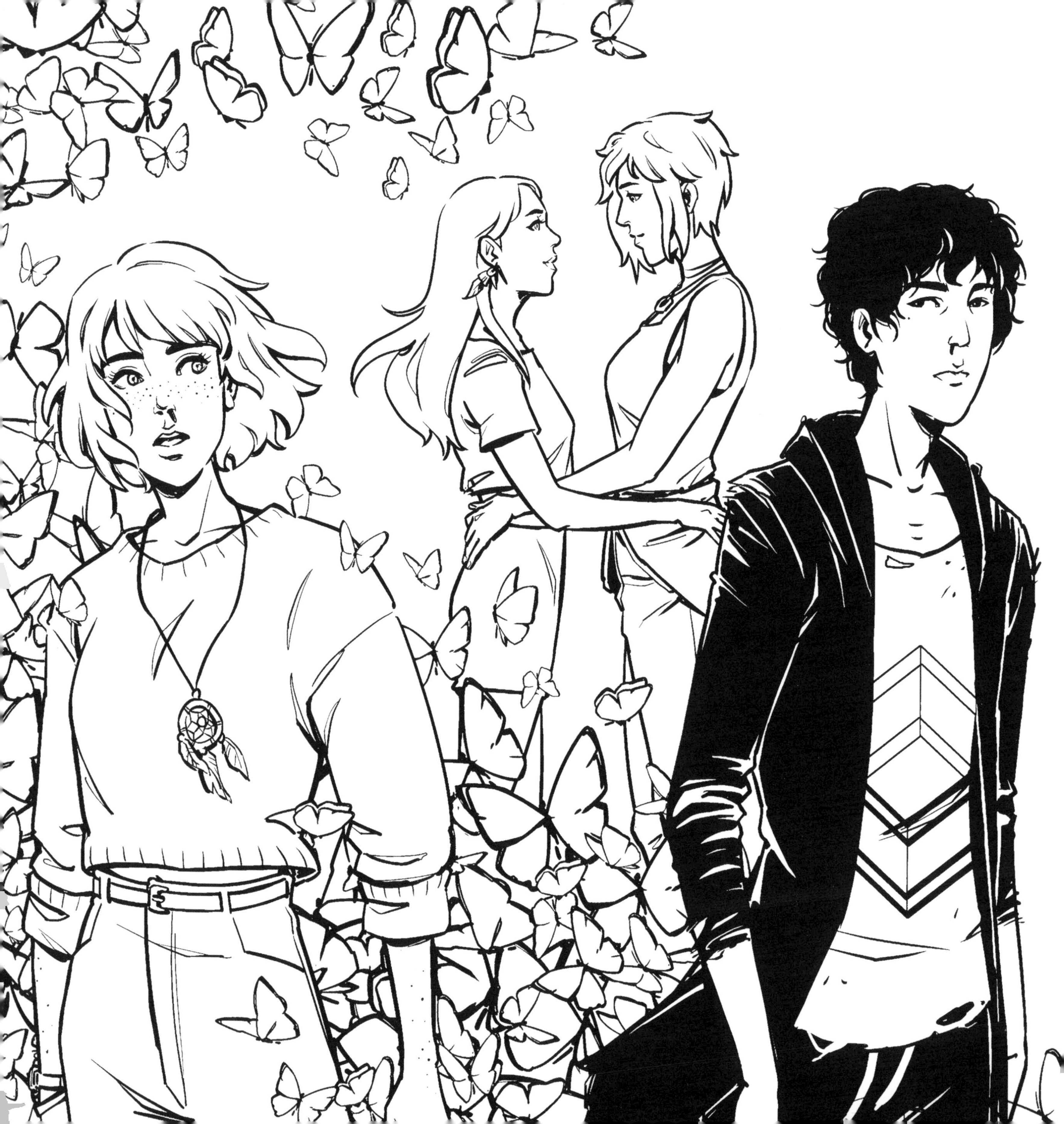

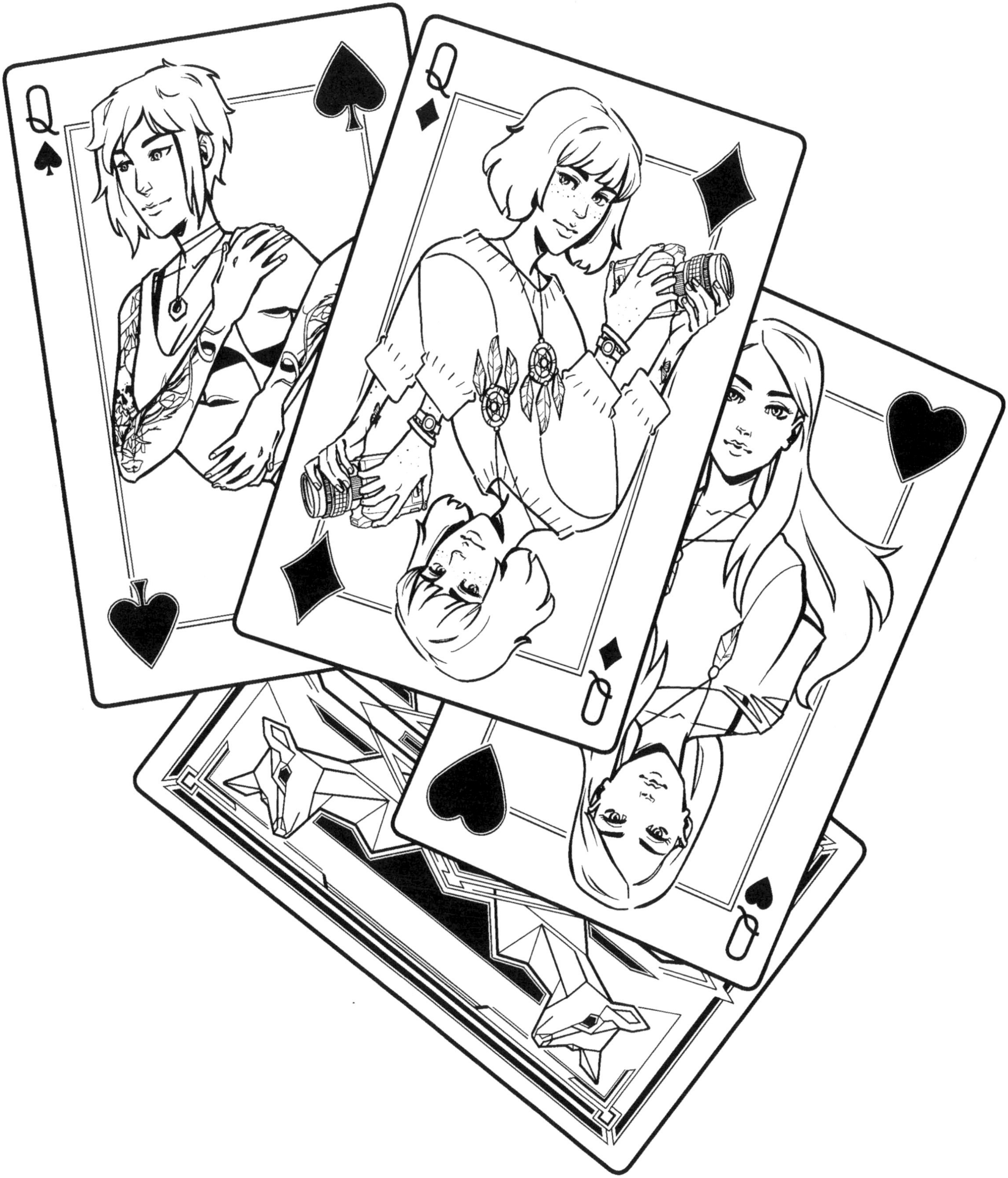

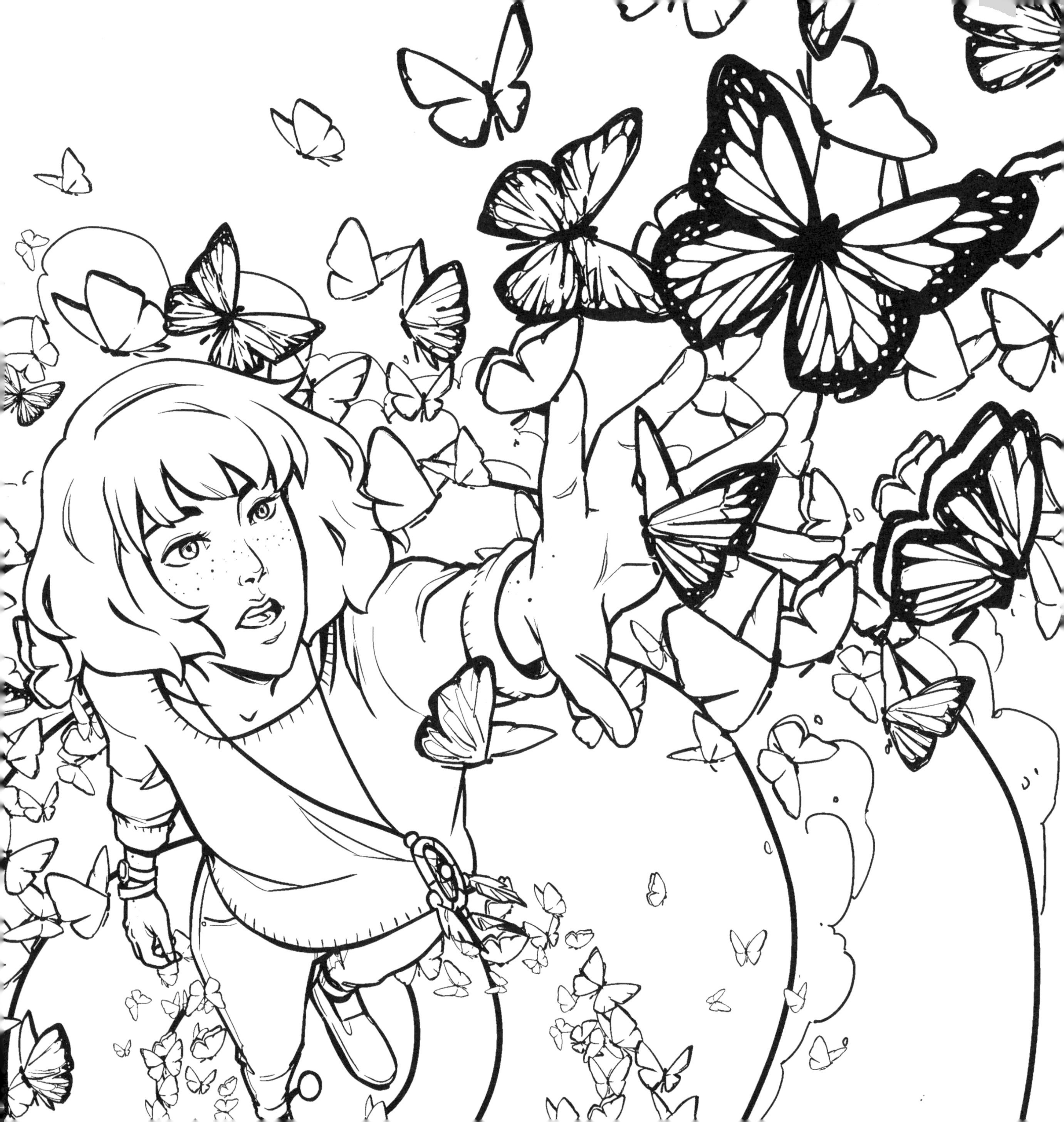

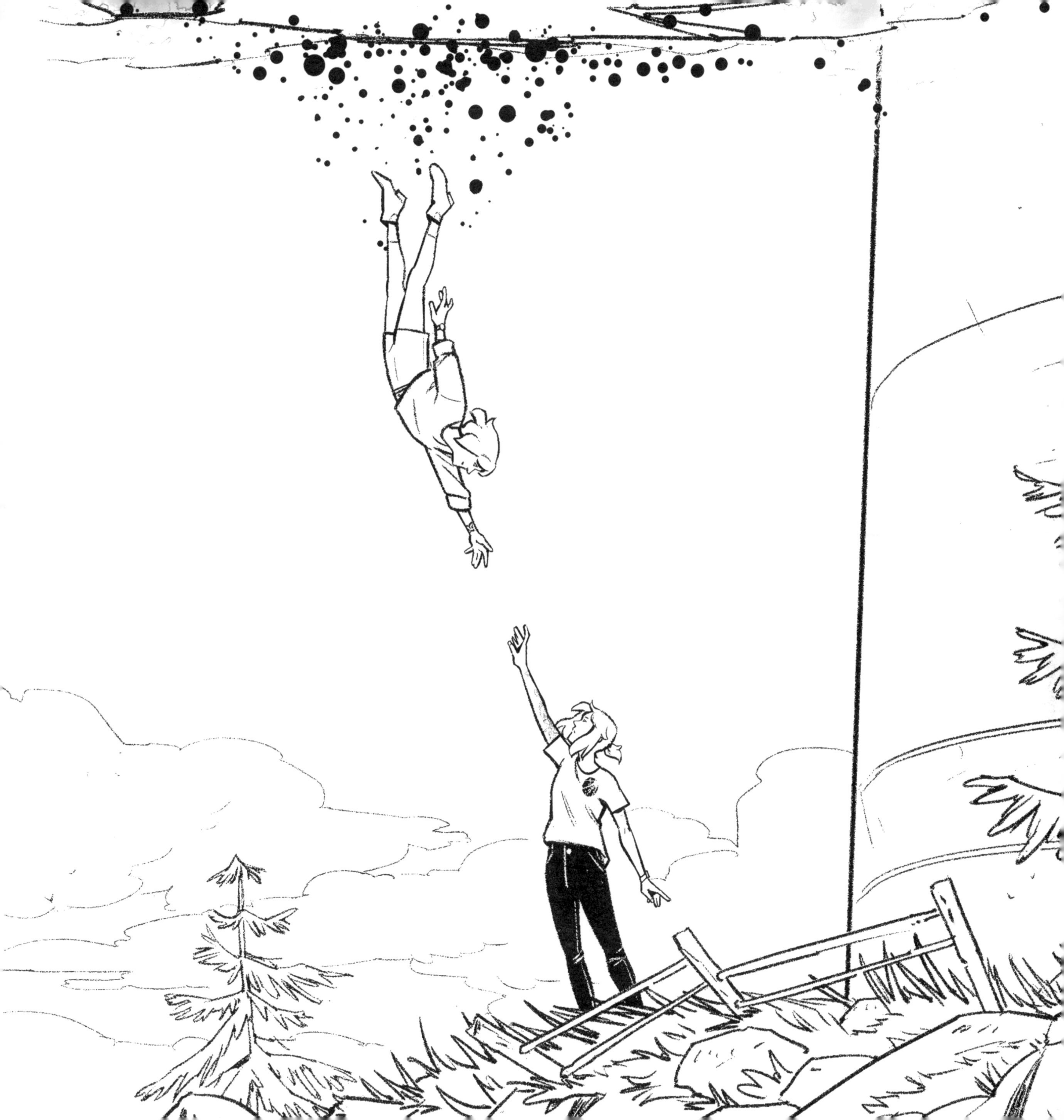

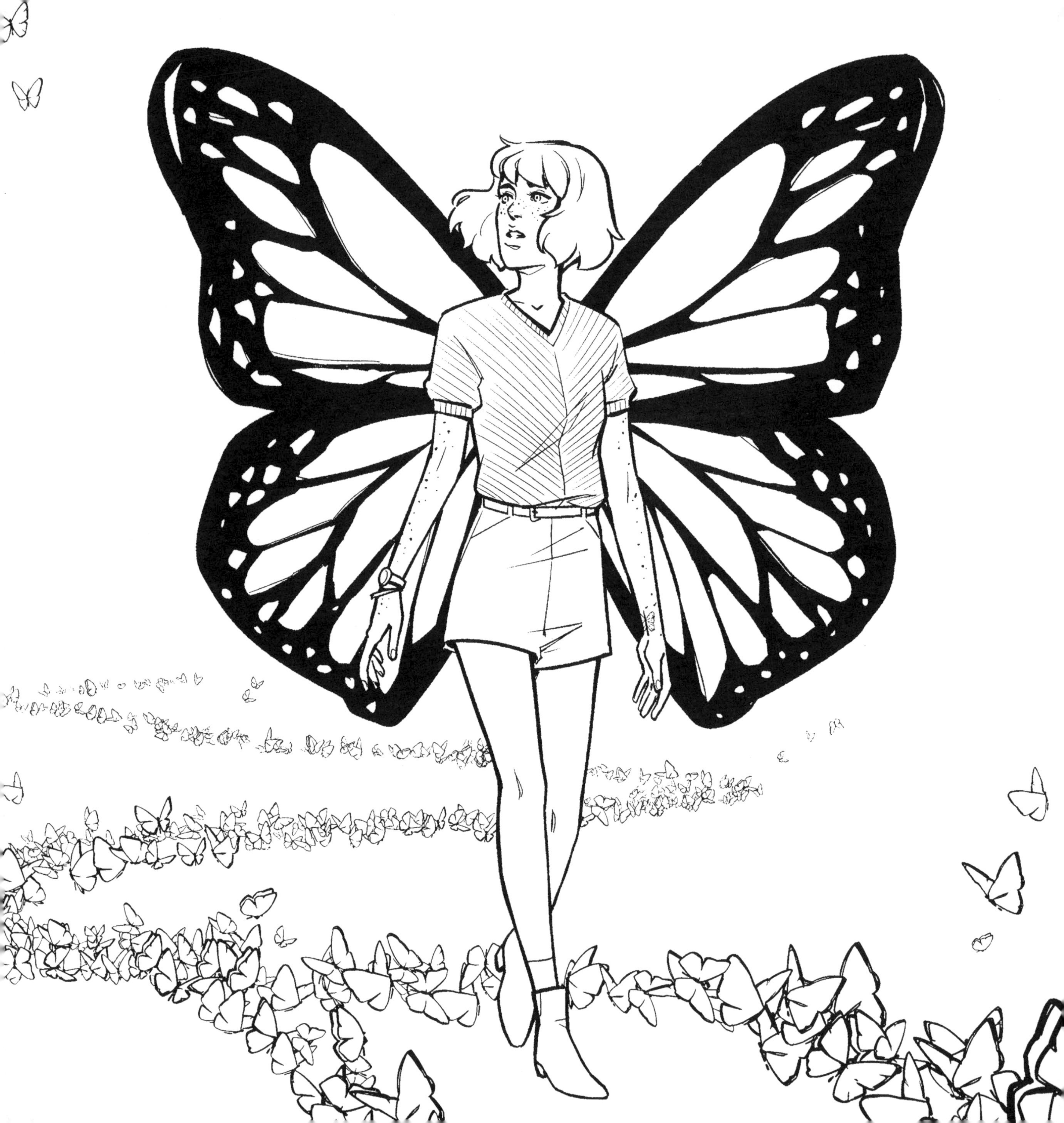

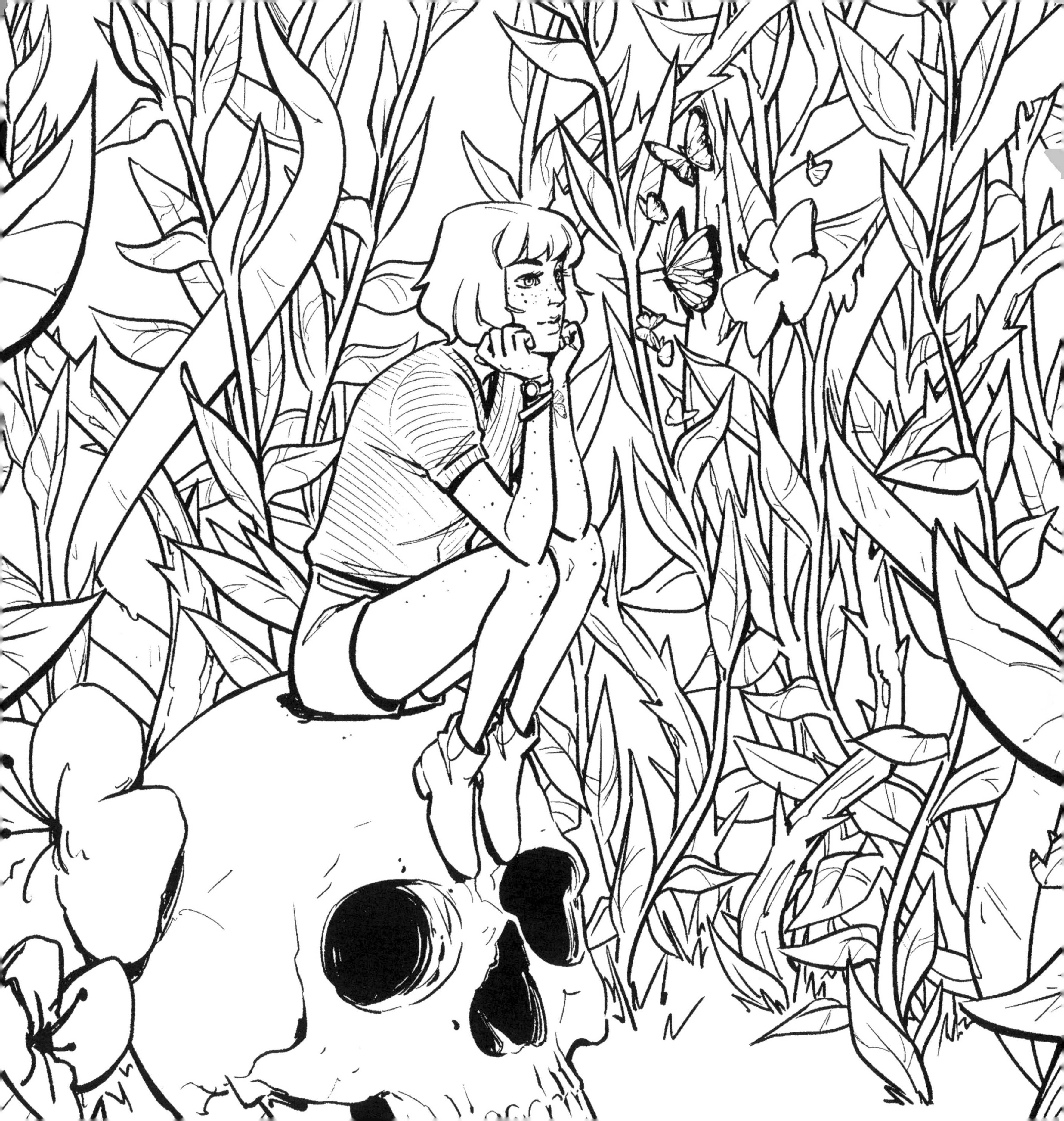

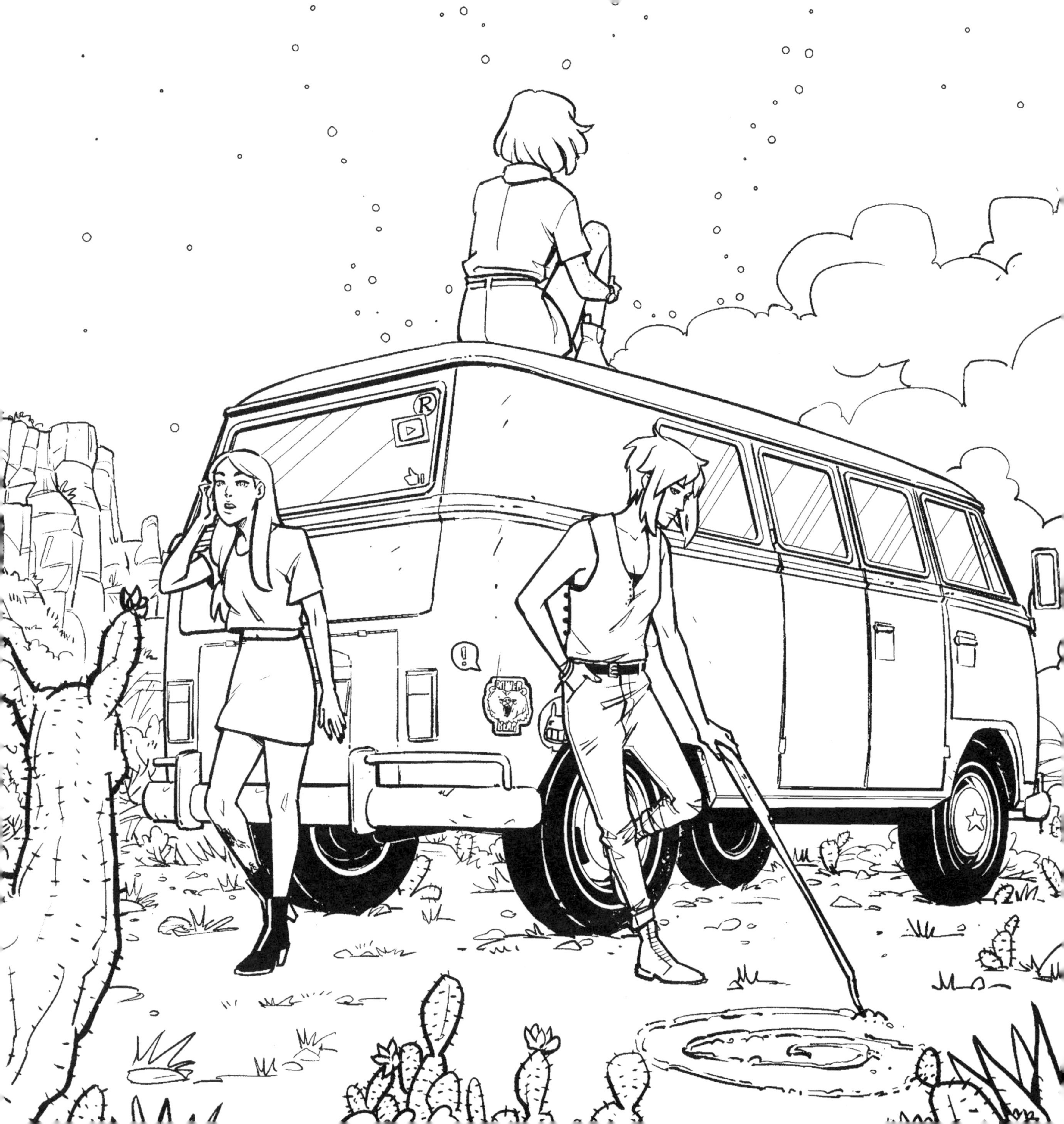
POWER BEAR

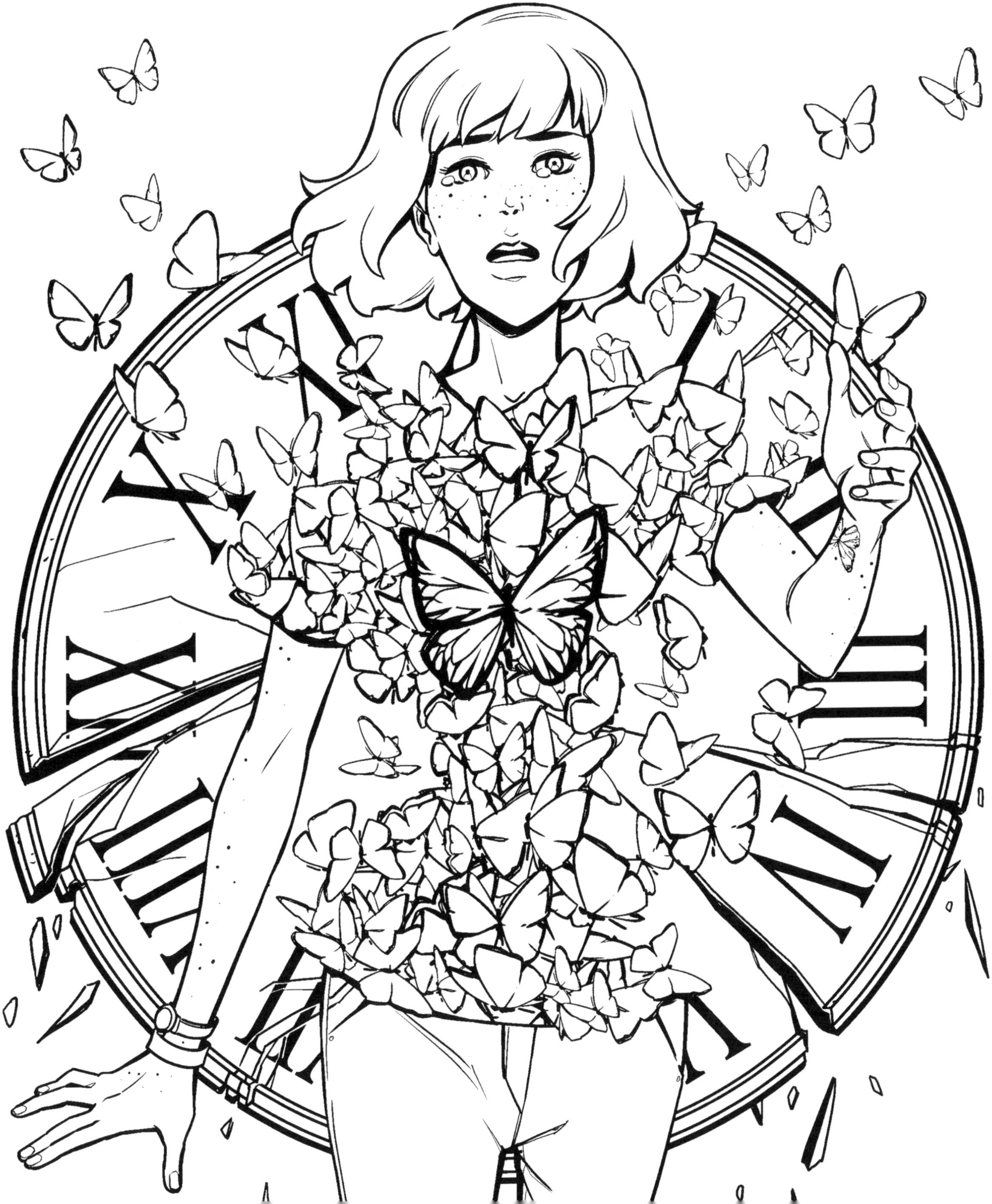

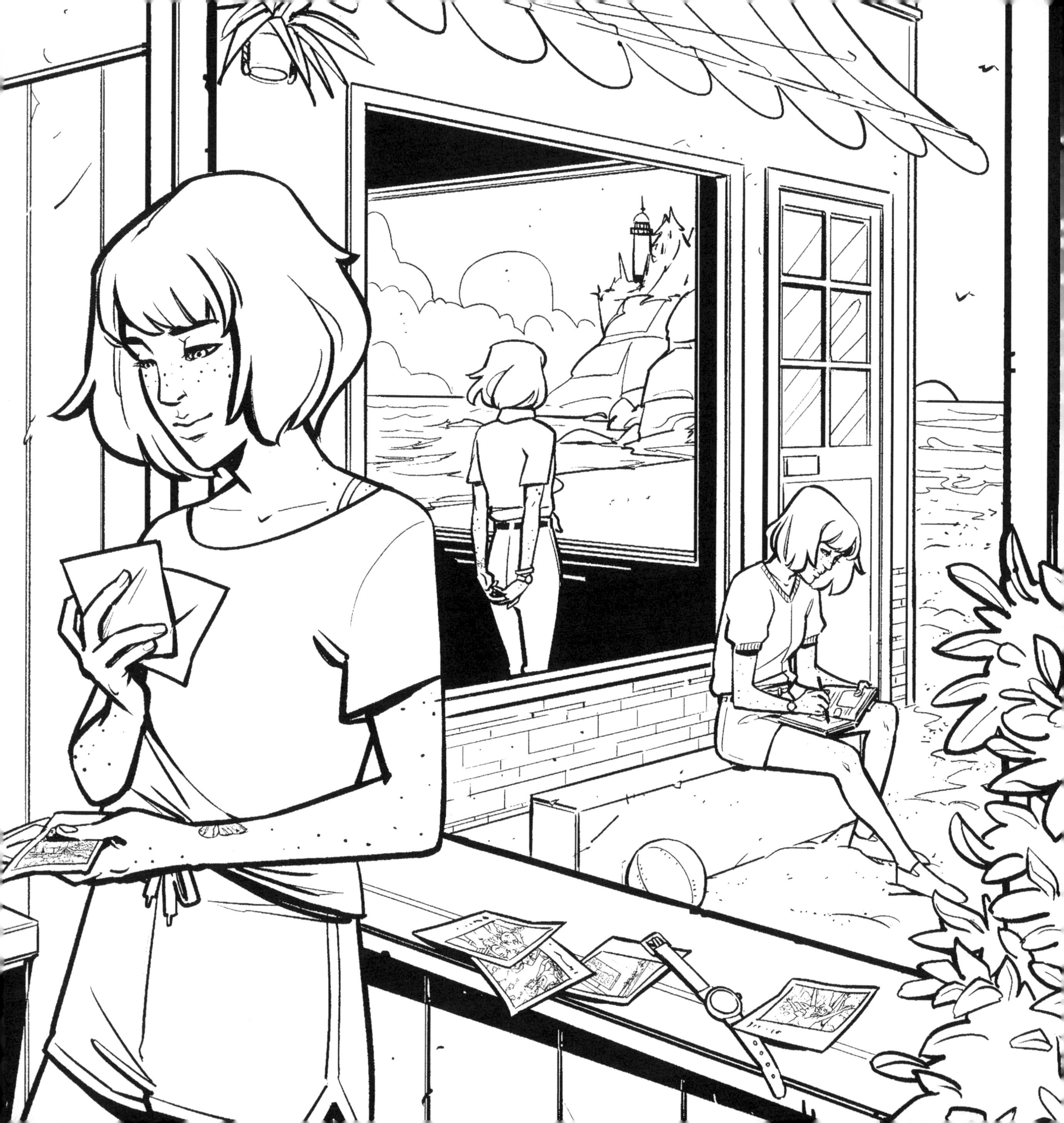

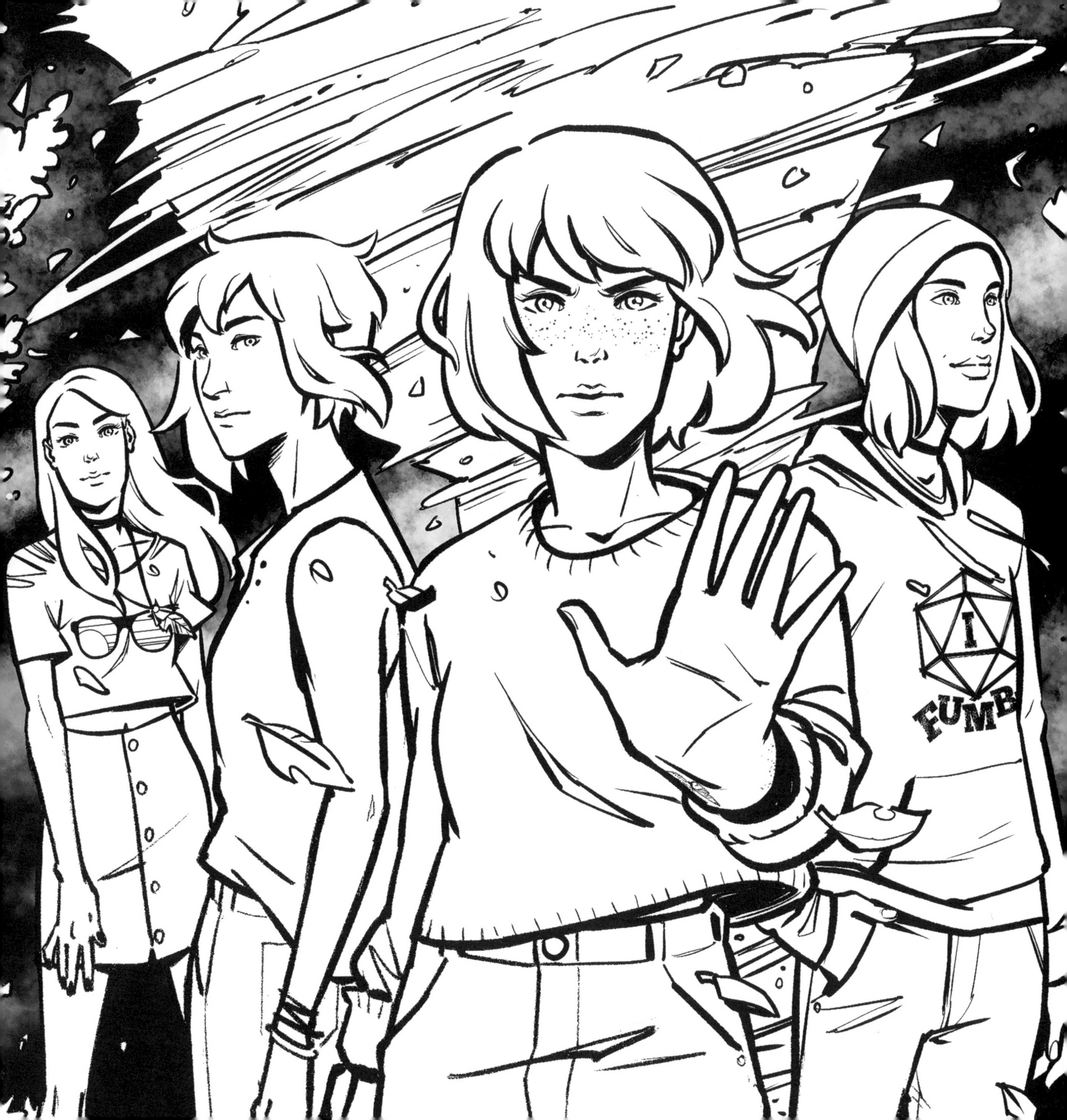
I
FUMB

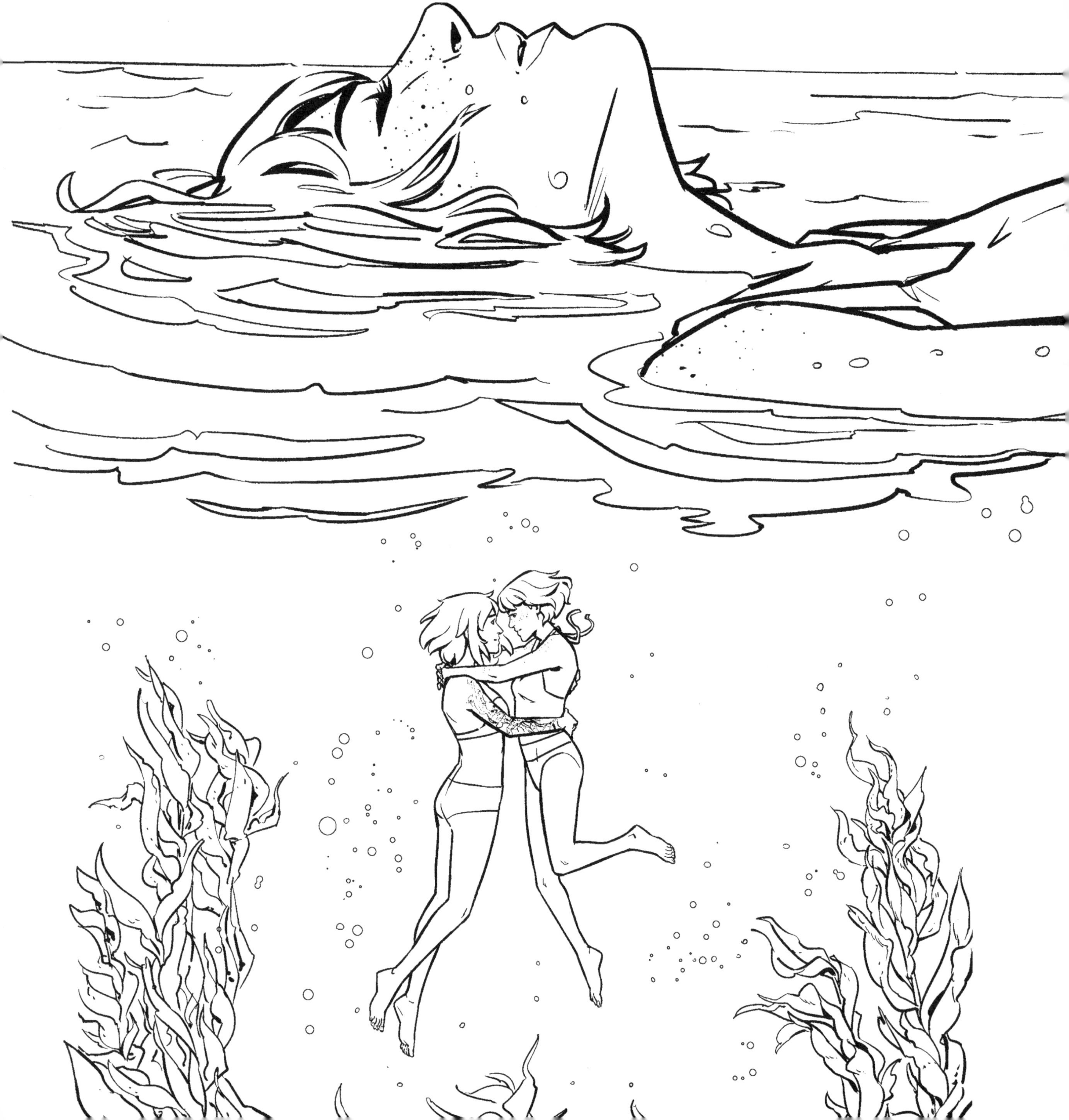

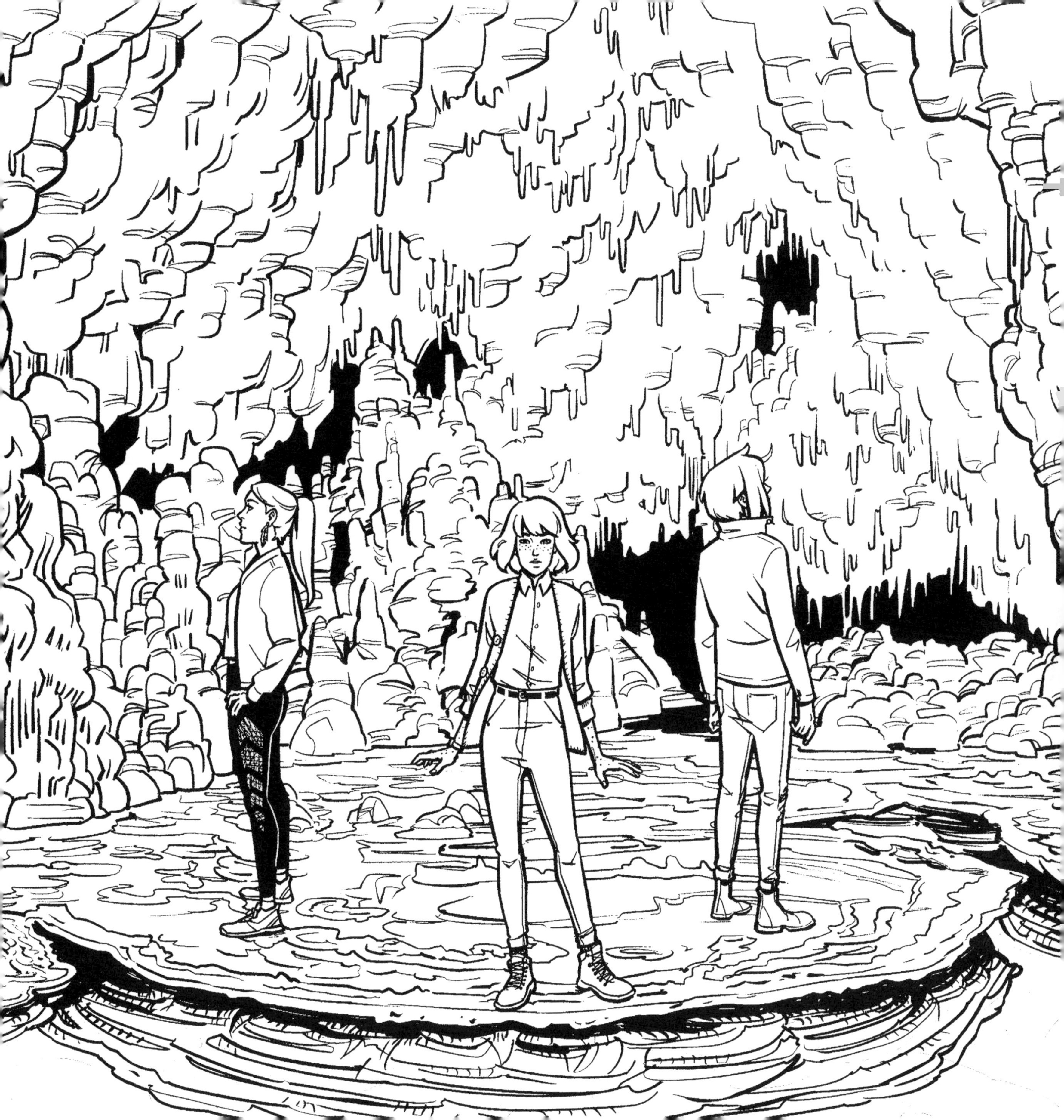

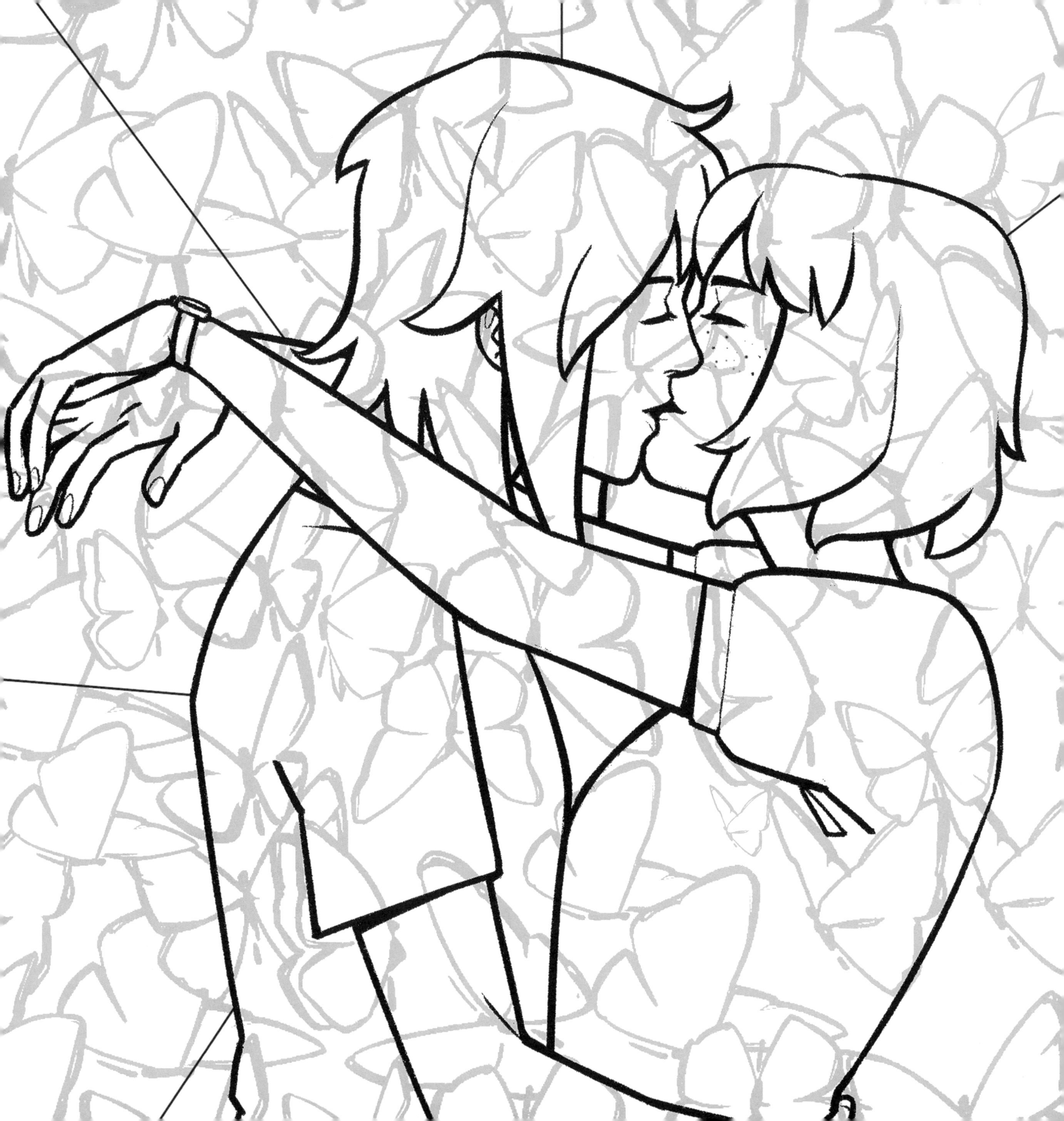

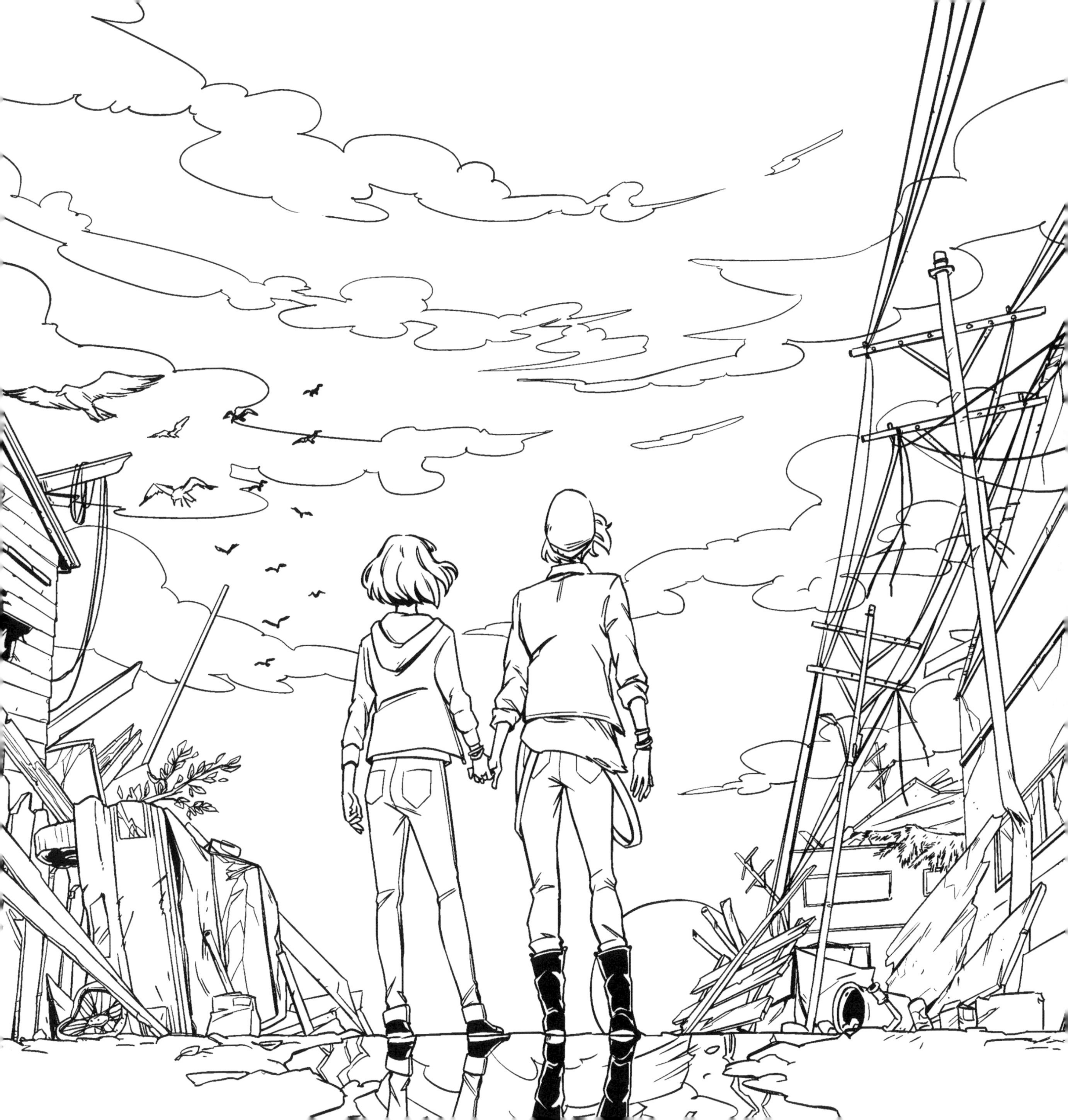

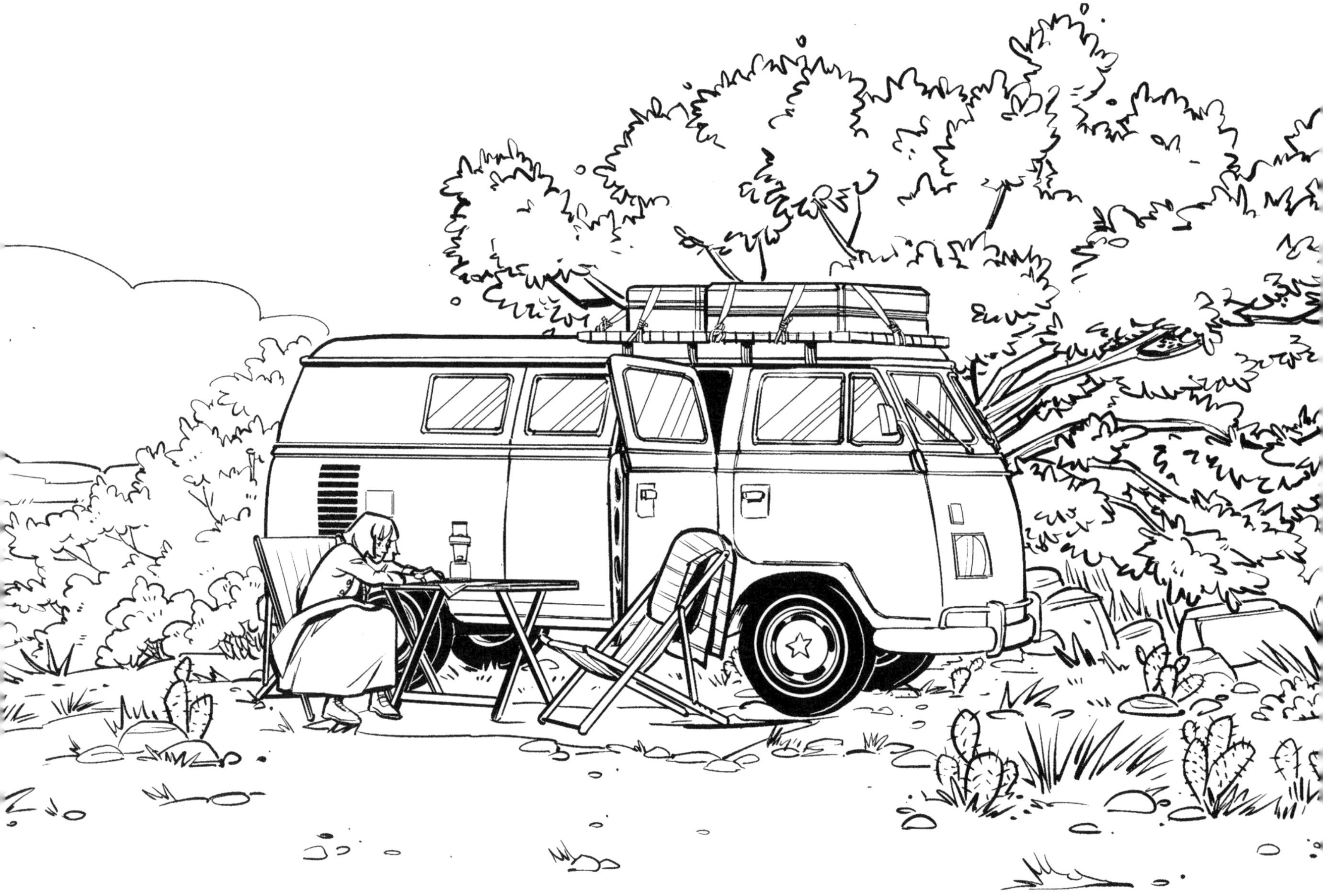

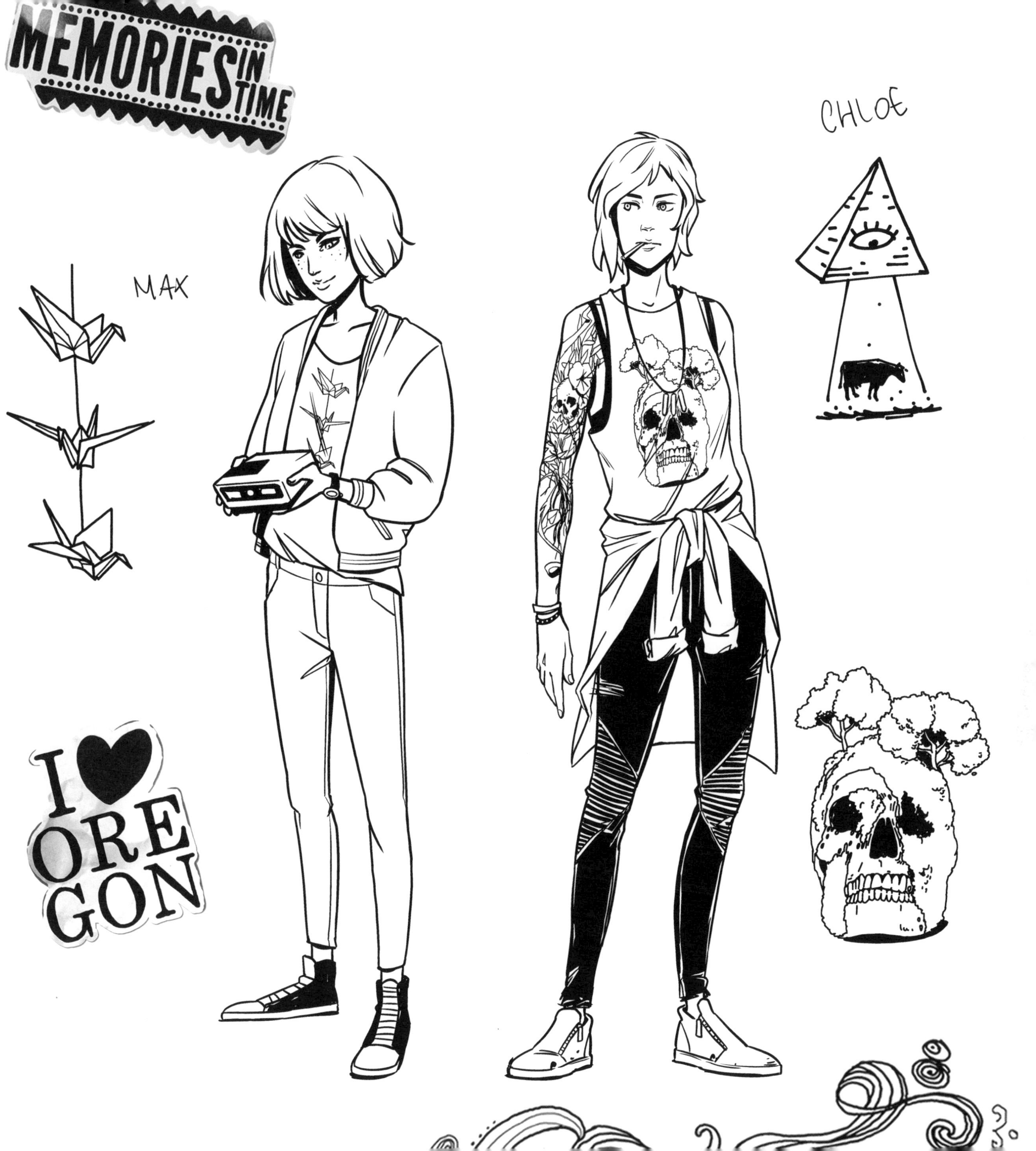
MEMORIES IN TIME
MAX
CHLOE
I ♥ OREGON

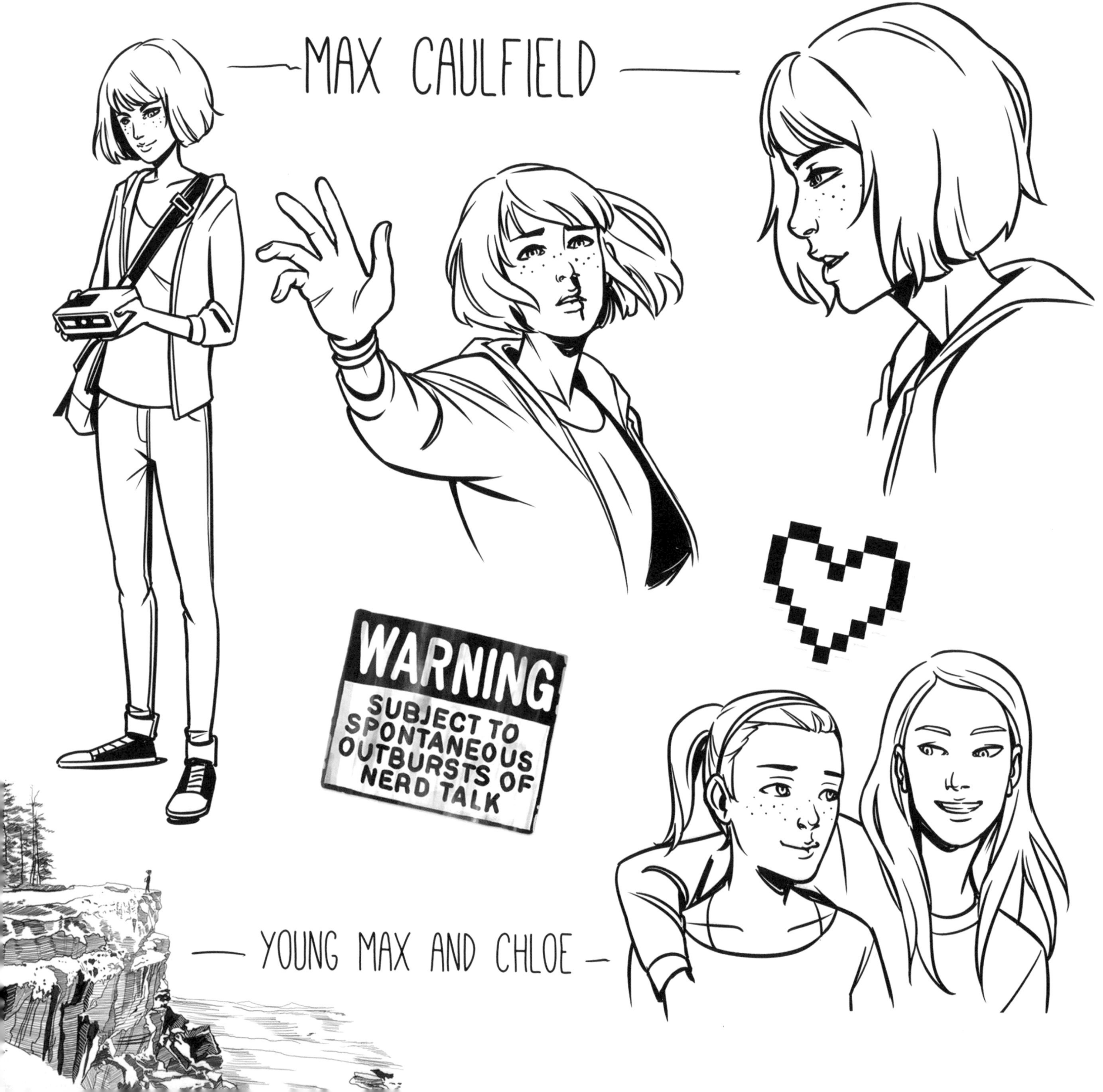
MAX CAULFIELD
WARNING
SUBJECT TO SPONTANEOUS OUTBURSTS OF NERD TALK
YOUNG MAX AND CHLOE

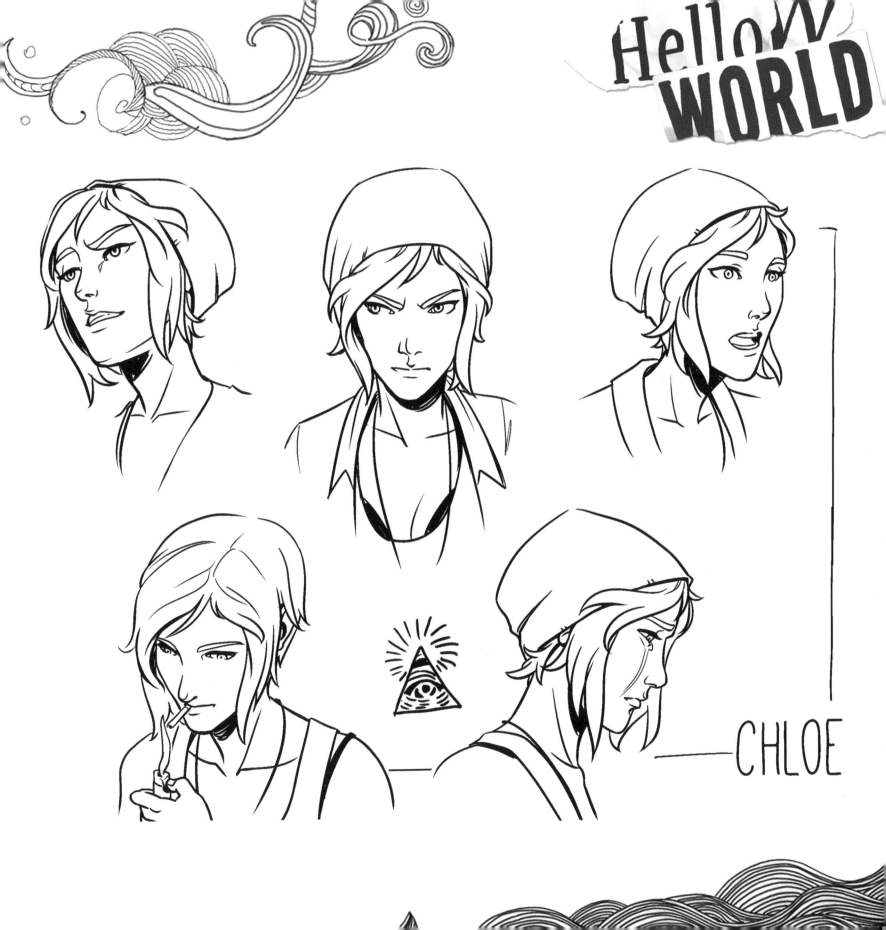

Hellow WORLD

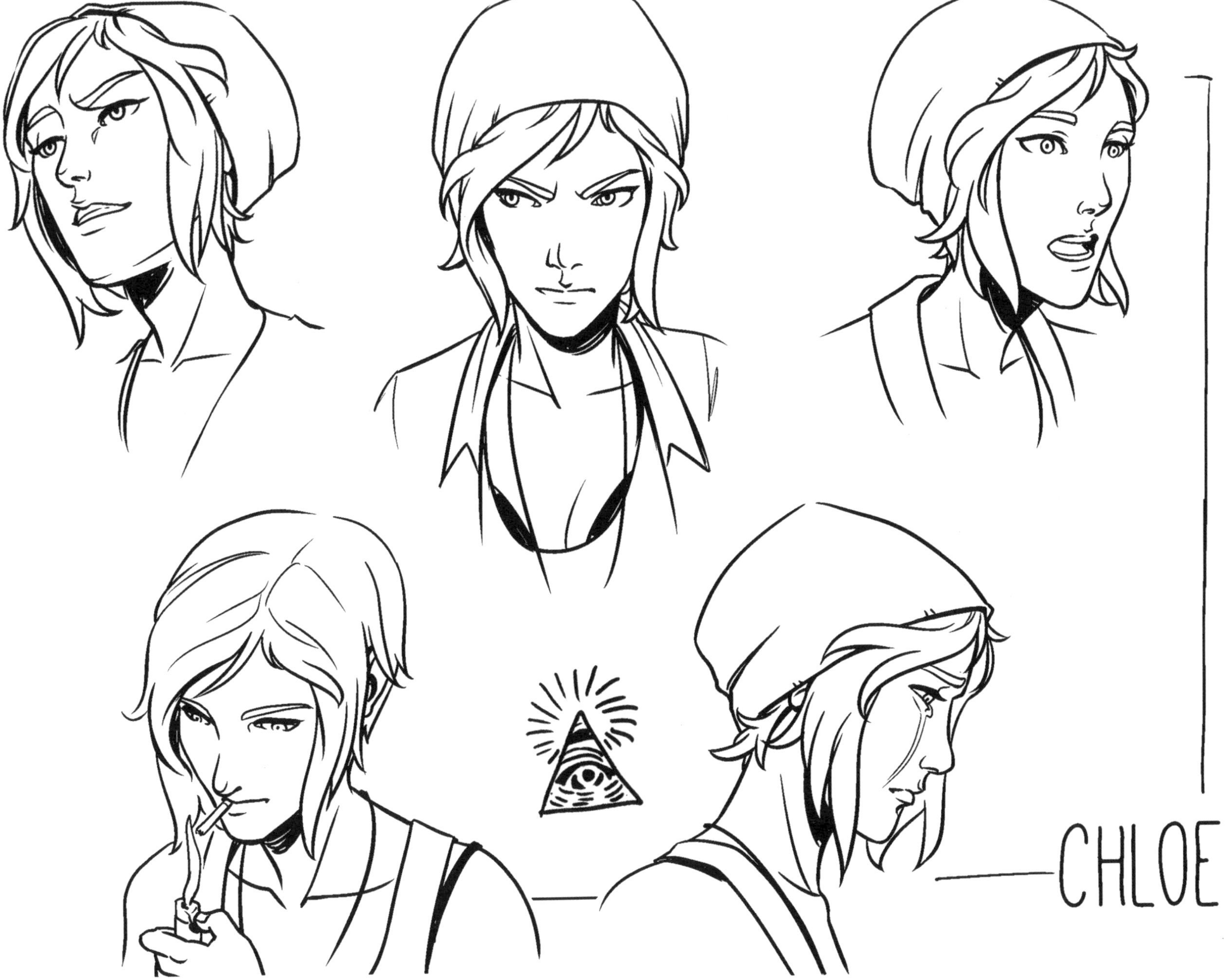
CHLOE

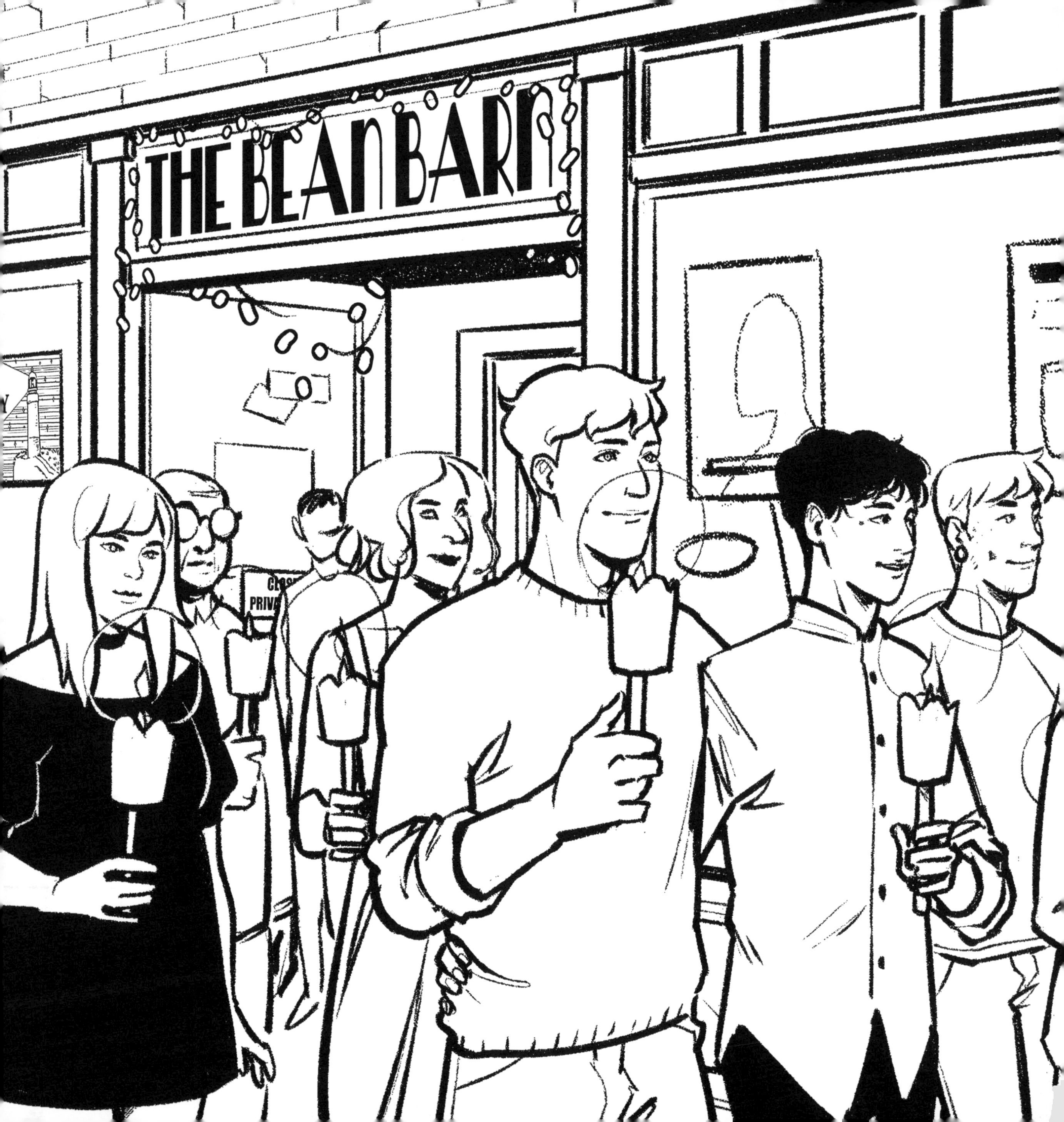
THE BEAN BARN

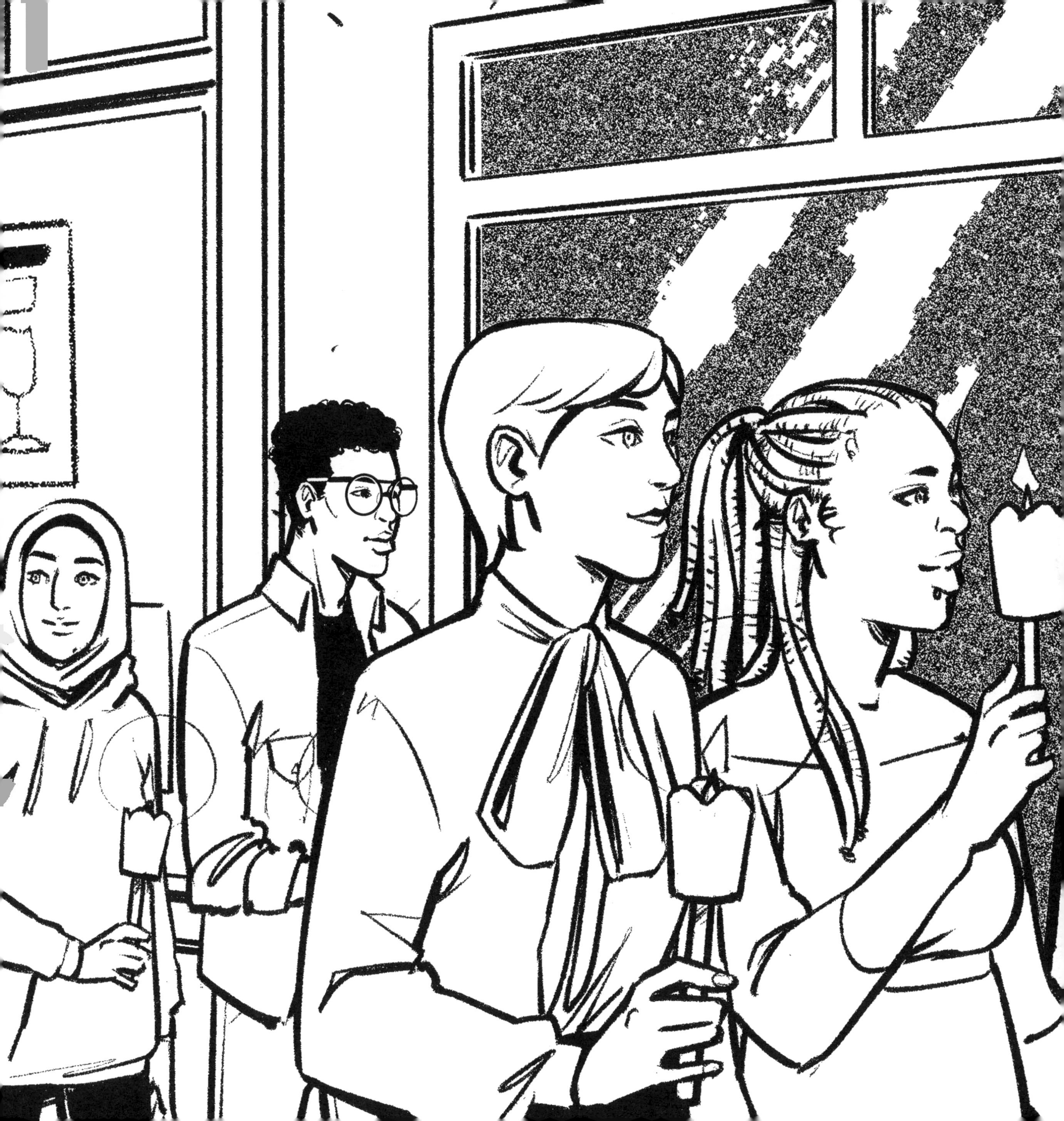

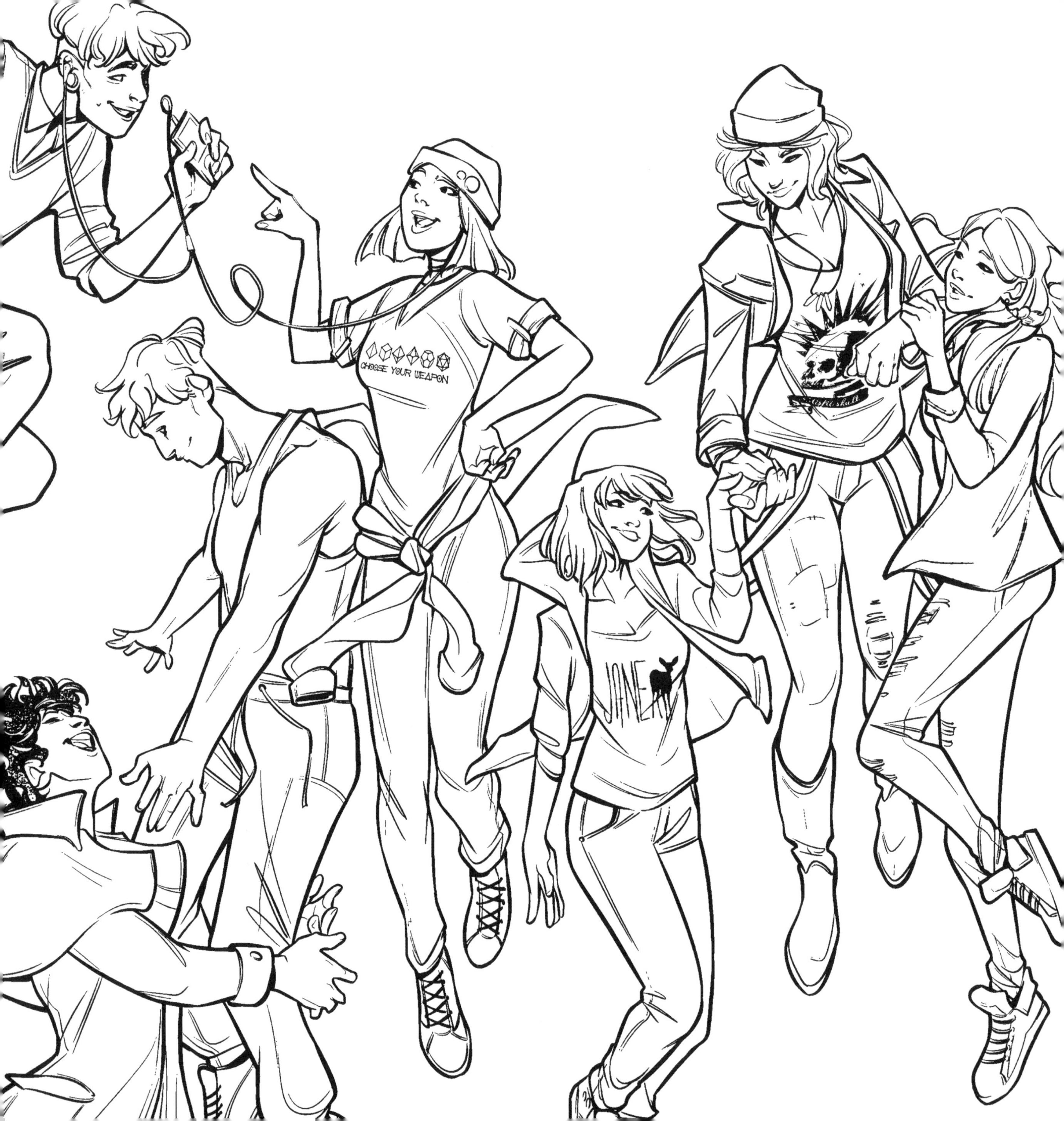
CHOOSE YOUR WEAPON
JANE

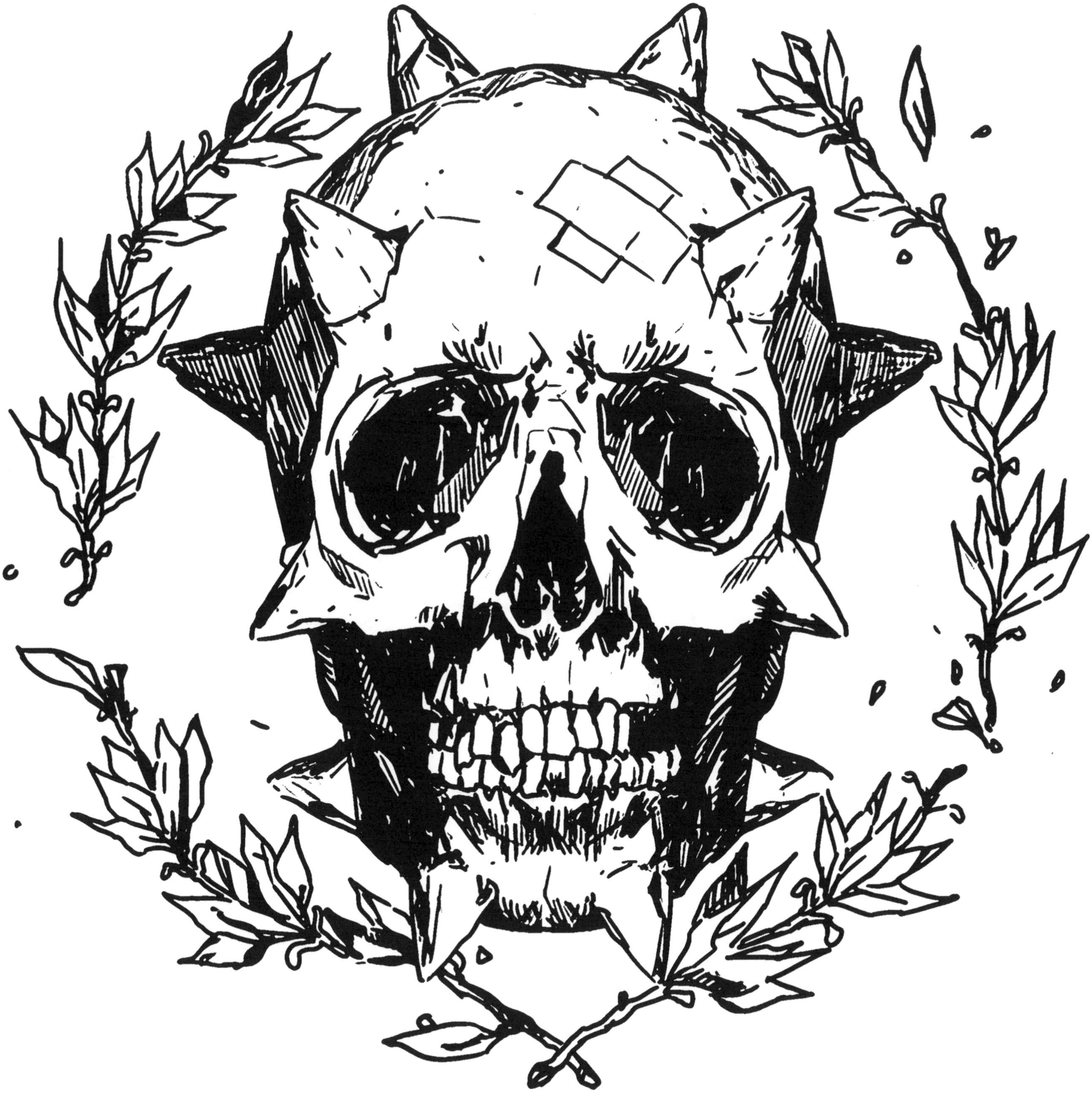

LIFE IS STRANGE

ART BY
CLAUDIA LEONARDI & IOLANDA ZANFARDINO

CLAUDIA LEONARDI is an Italian artist who dreamed of becoming a comic artist since she was a child. Circa 2012, she and Andrea Izzo met at the local comic school and joined forces to make their shared dream a reality. After working for Italian comic publishers on titles such as Bren Gattonero and Zeroi, plus indie productions as a penciller and inker, she made her international debut with *Life is Strange*.

IOLANDA ZANFARDINO is a comic book creator and cover artist currently working with Titan Comics and the creator of books such as *Hecate's Will*, *A Thing Called Truth* and *Alice in Leatherland*. After a long arduous "I'll do what I really love!" process, she finally works on queer (love) stories, and she's so excited she still can't even believe it. She likes rock musicals, street art, Pride parades, dystopian literature, and brave heart-warming comedies.